D1379759

INTEGRATION AND COMMUNITY BUILDING IN EASTERN EUROPE

INTEGRATION AND COMMUNITY BUILDING IN EASTERN EUROPE

Jan F. Triska, series editor

The German Democratic Republic

Arthur M. Hanhardt, Jr.

The Polish People's Republic

James F. Morrison

The Development of Socialist Yugoslavia

M. George Zaninovich

The People's Republic of Albania

Nicholas C. Pano

THE PEOPLE'S REPUBLIC OF ALBANIA

THE
PEOPLE'S
REPUBLIC OF
ALBANIA

NICHOLAS C. PANO

THE JOHNS HOPKINS PRESS

Baltimore

Manufactured in the United States of America

Library of Congress Catalog Card Number 68–27736

FOREWORD

he People's Republic of Albania is one of a series
of monographs dealing with integration and community building among the communist party states of
Eastern Europe. The studies of the East European
countries are part of a larger program of studies of the
world communist system sponsored by Stanford University.

It seems appropriate here to outline the theoretical
and methodological concepts that were developed for
the series as a whole. The focus has been on the world
communist movement as a system—its origins, development, and internal behavior. The major underlying
assumption is that each communist party state has
characteristics peculiar to it that predispose it toward
varying degrees of co-operation, co-ordination, and integration with the others. We think that the present
behavioral characteristics of the system can be traced to
environmental, attitudinal, and systemic factors, and
that we can learn a great deal from a comparative
analysis of the process and the degree of integration
of each member state into the system of communist
party states—whether, for example, the process involves
force or consent, similar or shared institutions and
codes of behavior, or whether integration is effective
at elite levels and/or at lower levels as well, and so on.

The concept of political integration and community formation and maintenance is, as a focus of intellectual curiosity and investigation, as old as the study of politics. The mushrooming of supranational integrational movements since World War II has given considerable new impetus to the old curiosity and has changed the emphasis of the investigations. Social scientists who in the last two decades have been building a general theory of political integration, whether on a subnational, national, or supranational level, have been perhaps less concerned with the philosophical content of the concept of integration than with discovering operational indicators that would endow the concept with empirical meaning and would allow the theory to be tested for validity and reliability. The principal centers of their inquiry have been two broad independent variables, *interaction* and *attitude*. Although in most cases investigated separately, interaction and attitude are assumed to combine to constitute a *community*, the *objective* of the *process* of integration.

The principal subjects of inquiry have been *transactions* across the boundaries of state units and *attitude formation* within the states. The theorists stipulate that numerous transactions are necessary for political integration and postulate that the densities of transactions among the units indicate their relationship. Flow of mail and telephone traffic; trade; aid; exchange of tourists, officials, and migrants; cultural exchange of persons and communications; newspapers, periodicals, and book sales and translations, radio, TV, and motion picture exchange; mutual treaties and agreements; and common organizations and conferences are the kinds of indicators that, measured and plotted over time, should demonstrate the direction of integrational trends and developments.

With reference to *attitude formation,* theorists have been more concerned with the process of integration than with its results (conditions) within states. The pertinent literature yields relatively little on this subject. In *Nationalism and Social Communication* Karl Deutsch argues that it may be fruitful to study two sets of persons within a unit of analysis: those "mobilized" for integrational communications and those "assimilated" into the new, larger unit. If those assimilated multiply at a more rapid rate than those mobilized, then "assimilation" is gaining and "community is growing faster than society."

At present enormous problems are involved in studying the *results* of the integration process in communist countries. It is difficult to assess attitudes because of the great sensitivity of officials and decision makers, and it is either difficult or impossible to get reliable aggregate and survey data. This informational problem makes it correspondingly difficult to develop a general theory of integration as well as to make systematic comparative analyses. We have therefore been compelled to rely on indicators of degrees and trends, indicators which depend considerably on subjective judgment and inference.

Although the data available are uneven in quality and quantity, our approach has been rigorous and systematic. Each author was asked to examine the country under review with reference to five historical periods: (1) the pre-communist stage before the country became a party state and hence a member of the system; (2) the period of the communists' consolidation of power after World War II when the states of

Eastern Europe entered the system; (3) the subsequent era of repression and rigid controls; (4) the period of relaxed controls following Stalin's death; (5) the last ten years. For each of these periods, as appropriate, the author was asked to identify and analyze the phenomena relevant to his country's integration in the system, its ecological-physical features, its demographic structure, belief system, social system, degree of autonomy, its dependence on other states, and its hopes, needs, and expectations with regard to integration and development. Within these broad confines, each author was asked to emphasize the periods and events with the greatest significance for the integrational development of the country in question. It is our feeling that a more rigid set of prescriptions would have been self-defeating in view of our objectives and the exploratory nature of our undertaking.

Although the principal purpose of Professor Pano's study is to examine the role of Albania in the world communist system, this monograph, thanks to the wealth of data and the historical scholarship the author brought to bear on the subject, can also serve as a useful introduction to the politics of Albania. Still, as in the other studies in this series, the major focus here is on that behavior of the People's Republic of Albania relevant to integration and community formation with its neighbors, with the Soviet Union, with China, and with other communist party states.

Albania, the People's Republic of "Eagles' Country" (Shqipëria—Republika Popullore e Shqipërisë) is about the size of Maryland with about half its population. Among the communist party states it is the smallest in territory (11,097 square miles), second smallest in population (almost 2,000,000) before Mongolia, and one of the poorest and most backward.

Darkly Stalinist at home and fiercely communist-independent abroad, Albania today, more than any other party state, reflects all the inherent insecurity of a small state desperately determined to go it virtually alone. It is not, and does not want to be, as its neighbors and critics in Eastern Europe claim, simply a Chinese colony on the Adriatic coast. True, listening to Radio Tiranë in Belgrade, Budapest, Prague, or Warsaw, one can scarcely escape the impression that this is Peking speaking: the particular language, style, form, and invective are all there. And like the Chinese leaders, the Albanian party chiefs are competitive, quarrelsome, and aggressive, irresponsible in their accusations and maladroit in their international behavior. But they are not simple marbles in a Chinese checkers game. The strange Sino-Albanian alliance is useful to both parties. As Professor Pano points out, Albania's break with the Soviet Union crippled Albanian plans to construct and rapidly develop a socialist state; today, ninety per cent of Albanian trade is with communist states, with China accounting for the bulk of it. For her part, China, in view of mounting difficulties with Asian communist party states and parties, welcomes Albanian friendship in the world communist system, in Europe, and in the United Nations.

Still, the Chinese have been unable to match Soviet assistance to Albania, and the Albanians have been unable to solve their agricultural difficulties. Professor Pano rightly concludes that the troubles are far from over for the communist leadership. "Unless the Albanian rulers can come up with a solution to the economic problems confronting the nation, they will find their position becoming increasingly difficult." Albania may yet have to search for a way back to those communist party states which it despises and fears, but which it needs to make the grade as a socialist state, namely, the Soviet Union and Yugoslavia.

One final remark of a general nature is in order: this series is based on the assumption that although the countries of Eastern Europe are now gaining increasing freedom to conduct their own affairs, they do not reject the need for some association among themselves. For the communist parties in power in Eastern Europe, the idea of a world communist community united in opposing capitalism and in carrying out its historical destiny is real and necessary. They would find it instinctively repugnant, we believe, to do anything that would precipitate a final, total break with the world communist system.

The series is an intellectual product of many creative minds. In addition to the authors of the individual monographs—in this case, Professor Nicholas C. Pano—I would like to thank especially Professor David D. Finley of the Colorado College and Stanford University for his original contribution and assistance.

JAN F. TRISKA

Institute of Political Studies
Stanford University

CONTENTS

GENERAL INFORMATION

Pronunciation Guide

The following letters and combination of letters in Albanian are pronounced differently from their English counterparts:

Albanian	English Phonetic Rendering	Example
c	ts (ca*ts*)	Pogradec
ç	ch (*ch*urch)	Korçë
x	dz (a*dz*e)	Xoxe
xh	j (*j*ust)	Hoxha
dh	th (*th*ey)	Dhimitër
ll	ll (pu*ll*)	Lleshi
j	y (*y*et)	Jakova
y	u (French d*u*)	Myftiu
ë	e (t*e*rm)	Tiranë
gj	gy (ho*gy*ard)	Gjirokastër
q	ky (stoc*ky*ard)	Shqipëria

The People's Republic of Albania
Republika Popullore e Shqipërisë

Area: 11,097 square miles
Population: 2,000,000 (1968 est.)
Communist Party membership: 66,327 (1966)

Major Cities:	Population: (1965)
Tiranë (capital)	161,330
Durrës	49,770
Vlorë	48,360
Shkodër	48,140
Korçë	44,605
Elbasan	36,635

Population Distribution: 33% urban, 67% rural

Birth rate: 35 per 1,000 (1965)
Death rate: 9 per 1,000 (1965)

Total school enrollment: 429,263 (1965/66)
Higher education enrollment: 12,761 (1965/66)
Illiteracy rate (over 9 years old): 10% (1968 est.)
Daily newspapers (2): Combined daily circulation 87,000
Cinemas: 81 (1965)
Radio receivers: 82,233 (1965)
Public libraries: 25 (1965)
Number of physicians: 900 (1965)

Road network: 3,500 km (1965 est.)
Railroad network: 178 km
National income by sector (1960):
Industry, 44.2%; agriculture and forestry, 34.6%; construction, 10%; transportation and communications, 3.2%; retail and wholesale trade, 6.8%; other, 1.2%

Principal natural resources: Oil, chrome, copper, iron, nickel, coal, timber, water power.

Principal agricultural products: Meat, hides, wool, bread grains and rice, cotton, tobacco, sugar beets, sunflowers, fruits, vegetables, fodder, lumber

Foreign trade: (1964)
Exports, $59,924,000
Imports, $98,128,000
Total, $158,052,000

Principal trading partners: China, Czechoslovakia, Poland, German Democratic Republic, Rumania, Italy
Currency: Albanian Lek (5 leks = 1 U.S.$)

The People's Republic of Albania

1: ALBANIA IN THE PRE-ENTRY PERIOD

Geography

Albania, the smallest and least developed of the European communist party states, is located along the west central coast of the Balkan peninsula. Encompassing an area of 28,748 square kilometers (11,097 square miles),[1] Albania borders on Yugoslavia in the north and east and on Greece in the south and southeast. The Adriatic Sea bounds Albania in the west. Albania occupies a strategic position in southeastern Europe and this fact has played an important role in the history of the country.[2]

The southwestern tip of Albania lies along the eastern littoral of the Strait of Otranto, the gateway to the Adriatic and Mediterranean Seas and one of the major routes from Western and Central Europe to the Near East. At its narrowest point, in the vicinity of Vlorë, the Strait separates Italy from Albania by only

[1] *Anuari Statistikor i R.P.Sh., 1961* ("Statistical Yearbook of the A[lbanian] P[eople's] R[epublic], 1961") (hereafter cited as *Anuari Statistikor, 1961*). Tiranë: Drejtoria e Statistikës, 1962), p. 3.

[2] Richard Busch-Zantner, *Albanien, Neues Land in Imperium* (Leipzig: Wilhelm Goldmann Verlag, 1939), pp. 163–68; Julian Amery, *Sons of the Eagle* (London: Macmillan and Company Ltd., 1948), pp. 1–5.

47 miles. A power which controlled the approaches to the Strait thus commanded one of the principal arteries from Europe to the East. The domination of Albania has therefore been the objective of the various powers which have sought to establish their hegemony in the Balkans and eastern Mediterranean from the time of the Romans.[3]

In addition to influencing the external relations of Albania, geography has also played an important role in the internal development of the country. Albania is predominantly a mountainous country with approximately 70 per cent of its area lying above the 1,000 foot contour line. The remaining 30 per cent consists of a coastal plain (which until recently was largely swamp or marsh land), rolling hills, and mountain and river valleys. In much of Albania the soil is of poor

[3] For general surveys of Albanian history, see L. S. Stavrianos, *The Balkans Since 1453* (New York: Rhinehart, 1958), pp. 496–512, 709–31; Stavro Skendi, ed., *Albania* (New York: Frederick A. Praeger, 1956), pp. 1–30; Robert Lee Wolff, *The Balkans in Our Time* (Cambridge: Harvard University Press, 1956), pp. 25–31, 91–95, 136–43, 147–50, 216–22, 232–34; Athanas Gegaj and Rexhep Krasniqi, *Albania* (New York: Assembly of Captive European Nations, 1964), pp. 13–39.

For more detailed accounts consult Stefanaq Pollo *et al.*, eds., *Historia e Shqipërisë* ("History of Albania") 2 vols. (Tiranë: Instituti i Historisë dhe i Gjuhësisë i Universiteti Shtetëror i Tiranës, 1959, 1965); T. Zavalani, *Histori e Shqipnis* ("History of Albania"), 2 vols. (London: Drini Publications, Ltd. [1957], 1966); Kristo Frashëri, *The History of Albania, A Brief Survey* (Tiranë: [The State Publishing House, "Naim Frashëri"], 1964); Joseph Swire, *Albania, the Rise of a Kingdom* (London: Williams and Norgate Ltd., 1929); Constantine A. Checkrezi, *Albania Past and Present* (New York: The Macmillan Company, 1919); Christo A. Dako, *Albania, the Master Key to the Near East* (Boston: E. L. Grimes Company, 1919); Ludwig von Thallóczy, ed., *Illyrisch-Albanische Forschungen*, 2 vols. (Munich and Leipzig: Verlag von Duncker und Humblot, 1916); Roland Bernard, *Essai sur l'histoire de l'Albanie moderne* (Paris: Les Editions Domat-Montchrestien, 1935).

quality and the water supply only marginally sufficient. Consequently, by the early 1940s only 9 per cent of the total area of the country was under cultivation.[4]

The rugged topography also served to make communications among the various regions of the country—especially in the highlands of the north—exceedingly difficult and has hindered the development of interregional trade.[5] What little trade existed between northern and southern Albania was conducted mainly by sea. With the passage of time, owing to the lack of communication and a differing environment, divergences developed between the north and south in speech, customs, and world outlook. These distinctions fostered localism, retarded the growth of national consciousness, and created a minor integration problem for the Albanian government during the first years of independence.

The People

The Albanians are descendants of the Illyrians, an Indo-European people who entered the Balkan Peninsula during the first millennium B.C. They are divided into two groups, the Tosks and the Gegs. The Gegs inhabit northern Albania and Kosovo-Metohija, while the Tosks live in the southern part of the country and in scattered communities in northern Greece. The Shkumbi River serves as a natural boundary between the territories occupied by each of these groups. Of the two, the Gegs are the more numerous, and they ac-

[4] Skendi, *Albania,* pp. 31–47.
[5] Carleton S. Coon, *The Mountains of Giants: A Racial and Cultural Study of the North Albanian Mountain Ghegs* (Papers of the Peabody Museum of American Archaeology and Ethnology, Harvard University, vol. XXIII, no. 3) (Cambridge: Peabody Museum, 1950), p. 29.

count for almost 67 per cent of the Albanian population.[6]

The Gegs belong to that ethnic type which anthropologists call Dinaric, that is, "tall, convexed nosed, long faced."[7] Since most of the Gegs live in mountainous, almost inaccessible regions, they have managed until recently to preserve their racial purity and traditional way of life. Despite the fact that Albania has been overrun by foreign invaders on numerous occasions, the Gegs have continued to enjoy a large measure of political autonomy. They were divided into ten tribal groups whose organization in many respects resembled the old clan system of Scotland. Until the late nineteenth and early twentieth centuries the Gegs had almost no contact with the outside world or even with the Tosks. Hence, they tended to be reserved and opposed to any changes which might serve to disrupt their long-established pattern of life. Above all, they have resisted the attempts of the various Albanian regimes to bring them under the effective control of the central government.

The Tosks, who from an anthropological standpoint are less homogenous than the Gegs, are primarily of the Alpine type.[8] They are shorter than the Gegs, more round-faced, and lack the high-bridged nose which is characteristic of the Dinaric type. Before the communist takeover most of them were peasants who lived in small villages and worked on farms owned by Albanian or foreign landlords. Since the terrain of

[6] Skendi, *Albania*, p. 57.

[7] Carleton S. Coon, *The Races of Europe* (New York: The Macmillan Company, 1939), p. 601. For a more detailed discussion of the Gegs, see Coon's *The Mountains of Giants*.

[8] Coon, *The Races of Europe*, pp. 602–4.

southern Albania is less rugged than that of the north, the Tosks were subjected to a greater degree of foreign control than the Gegs. Nevertheless, the Tosks also were able to maintain their national identity and their contacts with non-Albanian peoples broadened their horizons. Around the turn of the century, some Tosks emigrated to other parts of Europe and to the United States, accumulated money there and returned home with a rudimentary knowledge of Western civilization. A few of them even sent their children abroad to study. Thus, what few foreign influences penetrated Albania usually entered by way of the south.[9]

During the interwar period the Albanian government attempted to extend its control over the Gegs by granting them state positions or pensions and by spending large (by Albanian standards) sums of money on public works programs and social welfare projects in northern Albania. These policies tended to annoy the Tosks, since they were taxed heavily and received few tangible benefits from the state. Some young Tosk intellectuals also resented the fact that they were unable to obtain civil service positions and that the underdeveloped state of the Albanian economy made it impossible for them to make full use of their education in their native land.[10] In desperation, a few of these young Tosks embraced communism. They be-

[9] G. D. L. Natchi, "Les facteurs impersonnels de la révolution albanaise," *Les Balkans*, III (December, 1932), pp. 214–15; Checkrezi, *Albania Past and Present,* pp. 195–97.

[10] League of Nations, Albania, *Report by the Commission of Enquiry on its Work from December 19th, 1922 to February 1st, 1923. The Enquiry in Southern Albania* (hereafter cited as *The Enquiry in Southern Albania*) (Geneva: n.p., 1923), pp. 9–10; Swire, *Albania*, pp. 404–9; Busch-Zantner, *Albanien, Neues Land in Imperium*, pp. 35–36.

lieved that Albania could not be transformed into a modern state unless the existing political, social, and economic systems were completely destroyed.

Religion

Another socio-cultural factor which influenced the development of Albania was the division of the country along religious lines.

When Albania gained her independence from Turkey, approximately 70 per cent of the population was muslim, 20 per cent (almost exclusively in the south) was orthodox, and the remaining 10 per cent (in the north) was catholic. The overwhelming majority of muslim Gegs were members of the orthodox Sunni sect, while the muslim Tosks were almost equally divided between the Sunnis and the more liberal Bektashi sect.[11]

Religious feeling and influence tended to be much greater in northern Albania than in the south. The muslim Gegs were for the most part fanatics, and they regarded Islam as an integral part of their way of life. The Roman Catholic Church, on the other hand, relied upon a vigorous missionary and educational program to maintain the allegiance of its communicants. Its European-educated clergy made valuable contributions to the Albanian intellectual and cultural revival of the nineteenth and twentieth centuries and strove to combat the spread of antireligious, materialistic ideologies into Albania.[12]

[11] Skendi, *Albania,* pp. 57–58, 286–92; Faik Konitza, *Albania: The Rock Garden of Southeastern Europe and Other Essays,* ed. G. M. Panarity (Boston: [Pan-Albanian Federation of America], 1957), pp. 131–44.

[12] For the role of the Catholic Church in combatting socialism and communism see Stafanaq Pollo, "Revolucioni i parë rus i

In the south the influence of religion was weaker than in the north. The Bektashi, for example, took a more liberal stand on social and political questions than did the Sunni. Indeed, members of the Bektashi sect played a prominent role in the Albanian national movement and were far more anxious to break all ties with the Ottoman Empire than the conservative Sunni. The main strength of the Albanian Orthodox Church lay in the fact that it served as an agency of Albanian nationalism. For the most part, the orthodox clergy were uneducated and did not command the respect of the small, but influential, educated middle class in this region. Religion, therefore, did not pose as serious a barrier to the propagation of liberal and even communist ideas in southern Albania as it did in the north.[13]

Yet despite the differences which exist between the Gegs and the Tosks, Albania is one of the most ethnically homogeneous states in Europe. These two Albanian groups account for 98 per cent of the population of the nation. The only important minority group in the country consists of some 35,000 Greeks who reside in southern Albania. In addition, there are sev-

---

1905–1907 dhe lufta e popullit shqiptar për pavarësi" ("The First Russian Revolution of 1905–1907 and the Struggle of the Albanian People for Independence"), *Buletin për Shkencat Shoqërore* ("Bulletin of the Social Sciences") IX, No. 4 (1955), p. 6; "Influenca e Revolucionit të Madh Socialist të Tetorit mbi zhvillimin e lëvizjes revolucionar në Shqiperi" ("The Influence of the Great October Socialist Revolution on the Development of the Revolutionary Movement in Albania"), *Buletin për Shkencat Shoqërore*, IX, No. 2 (1955), p. 53.

[13] Jani I. Dilo, *The Communist Party Leadership in Albania* (Washington, D.C.: Institute of Ethnic Studies, Georgetown University, 1964), pp. 9–10.

eral thousand Vlachs, Bulgarians, and Serbs scattered throughout Albania.[14]

Demography

During the interwar period Albania had the highest birth rate in Europe, as well as one of the highest death rates, and her population rose from 803,959 in 1923 to 1,122,044 in 1945.[15] Almost 80 per cent of the Albanian people in 1945 were illiterate, were engaged in agriculture, and lived in small towns and rural settlements. As late as 1945 there were only three cities in Albania with a population of 20,000 or more.[16] Thus, the absence of a large urban industrial proletariat and a well-educated middle class, coupled with the existence of a massive, illiterate, apathetic peasantry, hindered the development of a strong communist movement in Albania during the interwar period.

Economy

The fact that Albania has never been a self-sustaining economic unit has played an important role in the history of the country. When Albania became an independent nation in 1912, her economy was the least developed of any state in Europe.[17] The principal com-

[14] Skendi, *Albania*, p. 57; Konitza, *Albania: The Rock Garden*, pp. 39–43.

[15] The Albanian birth rate in 1938 was 34.7 per 1000 while the death rate during the same year was 17.8 per 1000. *Anuari Statistikor, 1961*, pp. 53, 306–7.

[16] *Ibid.*, p. 53; Skendi, *Albania*, pp. 49–59.

[17] A summary of economic conditions in Albania prior to the communist takeover appears in United Nations, *Economic Survey of Europe in 1960* (hereafter cited as *ESE*, 1960) (Geneva:

ponents of the Albanian economy were a primitive self-sufficient agriculture and livestock raising. There was no industry worthy of mention. Interregional trade was virtually non-existent. There were only seven hard-surfaced roads with a combined length of 185 kilometers and only one modern bridge in the entire country. The Albanian economy in 1912 was not merely under-developed—it was undeveloped. World War I then intervened and little was accomplished until 1922, when Albania first asked the League of Nations for help.

In 1924 when Bishop Fan Noli seized power, he sought to finance his economic and social reform program by obtaining a loan from the League of Nations, but was refused. When Ahmet Zogu became president of Albania in 1925, he too realized that no significant economic development could take place without the support of one of the Powers. Zogu chose Italy. Be-

---

Secretariat of the Economic Commission for Europe, 1961), pp. 1–4. For a more detailed account consult Skendi, *Albania*, pp. 148–254 *passim*.

Excellent analyses of the Albanian economic situation during the first decades of independence appear in Albert Calmès, *The Economic and Financial Situation in Albania* (Annex to the Report presented to the Council by the Financial Committee on its Eighth Session) (Geneva: Imp. A. Kundig, 1922); Maxwell Blake, *Economic Conditions in Albania* (Washington, D.C.: U.S. Government Printing Office, 1923), pp. 1–10; Great Britain, Foreign Office, Historical Section, *Albania* (London: H.M. Stationery Office, 1920), pp. 80–90.

Two recent Albanian views are Harilla Papajorgji, *The Development of Socialist Industry and its Prospects in the People's Republic of Albania* (Tiranë: [The State Publishing House "Naim Frashëri"], 1962), pp. 3–20; and Theodhor Kareco, "Rreth zhvillimit të forcave prodhuese në industri gjatë viteve 1920–1940" ("The Development of Productive Forces in Industry During the Years 1920–1940"), *Studime Historike*, XIX, No. 4 (1965), pp. 81–108.

ginning in 1925 Albania and Italy concluded a series of economic agreements that resulted in the creation of an Italian-dominated Albanian national bank, and in the establishment of several Italian-controlled corporations to exploit Albania's natural resources and execute a public works program there. Other Italian corporations were later awarded concessions to develop Albanian industry and agriculture. In addition, the Italian government granted a number of loans to the Zogu regime during the late 1920s and throughout the 1930s. These were mainly used to offset the chronic Albanian budgetary and foreign trade deficits and were political rather than economic in character. Mussolini never really expected monetary repayment from the Albanian state, but he did demand political loyalty. In this manner Italy exercised a strong influence in the conduct of Albanian foreign policy.[18]

While Italy did make some significant contributions to the development of the Albanian economy between 1925 and 1943, it should be noted that the Italians were primarily interested in building up only those sectors of the Albanian economy which contributed to their own economic and military strength. Italy was especially anxious to increase the output of Albanian oil, chrome, copper, and iron ore. In agriculture the major emphasis was placed upon bringing more land under cultivation by reclaiming the swamp and marsh lands along the Albanian coastal plain. The Italians made little effort to build up Albanian industry. With the exception of the Shkodër cement factory, virtually all of the industrial enterprises established in Albania during the 1930s consisted of food processing plants

[18] Maxwell H. Macartney and Paul Cremona, *Italy's Foreign and Colonial Policy, 1914–37* (London: Oxford University Press, 1938), pp. 114–23.

and small factories specializing in the production of consumer goods. As late as 1938 industrial output in Albania accounted for only 4.4 per cent of the country's national income.

The Italians did, however, make a valuable contribution in the area of public works. They built over 1200 kilometers of new roads, constructed several hundred bridges, and improved the harbor of Durrës. In addition, they began to modernize the city of Tiranë by erecting government buildings, apartment houses, and several hotels.

Despite Albania's economic progress during the 1930s and 1940s, she was still the most backward state in Europe at the end of World War II. Agriculture had scarcely progressed beyond the primitive self-sufficient stage of 1912. There was still little industry worthy of mention. Much of the country's highway system and the port of Durrës lay in ruins. Thus, when the communists assumed control of Albania in 1944, they had to cope with the same economic problems the Albanian founding fathers had faced in 1912; and World War II had destroyed most of the gains that had been registered in industry and public works. Once again, foreign assistance was necessary for survival and development. Albania's economic dependence played an important role in governing her relations with the members of the communist system after World War II.

History

Modern Albania is located on the site of the ancient Kingdom of Illyria, which was conquered in 167 B.C. by the Romans who wanted to secure their position in the Adriatic. Having gained control of the Strait of

Otranto, they transformed the conquered Illyrian provinces into a base for imperial expansion into the East.

After the division of the Roman Empire in 395, Albania fell under the jurisdiction of the Eastern Empire. As the Byzantine Empire began to decline, Albania was subjected to a series of invasions by the various Slavic tribes which began to filter into the Balkans during the sixth century. These Slavic incursions resulted in the migration of Serbs, Bulgars, and other peoples into regions that had been almost exclusively inhabited by the Illyrians. While some of the Illyrians were absorbed by the Slavs, others moved southward and became concentrated in the Shkodër-Durrës-Ohër-Prizren quadrilateral. By the eleventh century these unassimilated descendants of the Illyrians were known as the Albanoi or Arbanitai (Albanians) and the region in which they lived was called Arbanon (Albania).

By the middle of the fourteenth century the hold of the Byzantine Empire on Albania had weakened to the point where several native feudal lords were able to establish their control over most of the country. After almost fifty years of intermittent warfare, the Ottoman Turks succeeded in conquering the Albanian states in 1431. Following the subjugation of Albania, the people continued to resist the Turks. It was not until 1444 that the Albanians found a leader, Gjergj Kastrioti (Skënderbeg), capable of uniting them in their struggle for independence. Between 1444 and the time of his death in 1468, Skënderbeg was able to free most of his homeland from Turkish bondage. After his death the Albanian resistance began to collapse and by 1479 the country had been restored to the Ottoman fold. Albania remained under Turkish domination for almost five hundred years. Except for some tenuous connections with the Papacy, Albania remained isolated from the mainstream of Western civilization until the late nineteenth century.

By the mid-nineteenth century the Albanian national renaissance was germinating. The first overt evidence of the nascent Albanian nationalist movement appeared in 1878 when a group of Albanian patriots formed the League of Prizren to prevent the partition of the Albanian provinces of the Ottoman Empire by the Congress of Berlin. Although the League failed to achieve this objective, its activities so disturbed the Sultan that he forced it to disband in 1881. Despite its brief life, the League played a major role in inspiring Albanian national sentiment and revolutionary activity.

Two major themes—the development of the Albanian national movement and the growing interest of the Great Powers in Albania—dominate the history of Albania between 1881 and 1912. During this period Albanian nationalist organizations and newspapers were established both in Europe and in the United States, with the aim of fostering patriotism and gaining foreign support for the creation of an autonomous Albanian state. At this same time Austria-Hungary, Italy, and Russia sought to incorporate Albania into their spheres of influence.

In 1908 the Albanians played an important role in the Young Turk Revolution, which resulted in the deposition of Abdul Hamid and the institution of a constitutional regime in Turkey. When the Young Turks proved to be as unsympathetic to the establishment of an autonomous Albania as the Sultan had been, the Albanians revolted. After four years of sporadic fighting, the Turkish government agreed in September, 1912, to create an autonomous Albanian state consisting of the provinces of Jannina, Monastir, Shkodër, and Kosovo. The future of the new Albanian state, however, was threatened by the outbreak of the First Balkan War in October. The Albanians realized that unless they disassociated themselves from the tottering Ottoman Empire, they would probably lose their newly won freedom. A national assembly of Albanian notables was therefore hastily convoked in the city of Vlorë and on November 28, 1912, it proclaimed the independence of Albania and established a provisional government under the leadership of the venerable patriot Ismail Qemal Vlora.

Albania sought immediate recognition of her independence from the Conference of Ambassadors then meeting in London to frame a peace settlement in the Balkans. Austria-Hungary and Italy favored the establishment of an ethnic Albanian state, which would have included most of the province of Kosovo within its frontiers. When Russia objected to the Austro-Italian proposals, it was decided on December 17, 1912, to recognize the independence of Albania and to determine the boundaries of the new state at a later date. While the Powers debated the Albanian boundary question, the country was overrun by Serbia and Montenegro in the north and by Greece in the south.

On March 22, 1913, the Powers finally reached an agreement concerning the northern boundary of Albania. The city of Shkodër, coveted by Montenegro, was awarded to Albania, but the province of Kosovo was assigned to Serbia. The Albanian-Serbian frontier of 1913 was virtually identical with the present frontier between Albania and Yugoslavia. As a result of this boundary settlement, over half a million Albanians were incorporated into Serbia and later Yugoslavia. The existence of this substantial Albanian minority in

Yugoslavia has been a constant source of friction in the relations between these states since 1913.

In the south, the determination of the Greek-Albanian boundary was complicated by the demand of the Greek government that Northern Epirus (the region which today includes the Albanian districts of Korçë and Gjirokastër) be awarded to Greece. The Great Powers finally decided in December, 1913, to permit Albania to retain control of the disputed region. The Greek government refused to accept the decision of the Powers and continued to encourage the activities of the irredentist Epirotes, who were seeking to unite Northern Epirus with Greece by means of force.

Following World War I, Albania escaped partition at the Versailles Conference largely as a result of President Wilson's intervention. The Albanian question was finally decided in 1921 by the Conference of Ambassadors, which reaffirmed the country's 1913 boundaries. After four years of political instability, Ahmet Zogu was proclaimed President of Albania. Three years later he transformed Albania into a hereditary "constitutional" monarchy and became the country's first king, assuming the title of Zog I, King of the Albanians. In the mid-1920s Zogu had turned to Italy for economic and political support. By the end of the 1920s Albania had become an Italian satellite.

During the 1930s King Zog on several occasions tried to break the Italian stranglehold on Albania. In each instance, however, he was forced to back down when Italy applied diplomatic, economic, and even military pressure. By 1938 the Italian government had become impatient with Zog's tactics and was anxious to assume direct control of the country. On April 7, 1939, the Italian army invaded and occupied Albania.

17

Albania now became a base for future Italian expansion into the Balkans. In October, 1940, Italy attacked Greece to "liberate" the "mistreated" Albanian minority in the northern Greek district of Çamëria. When the Greeks pushed the Italians back into Albania during the winter of 1940–41, they were greeted as liberators by the people. Albanian support for the Greek cause soon evaporated, however, when the Greeks announced their intention of annexing Northern Epirus. After the German intervention in the Balkans and the capitulation of Greece and Yugoslavia in April, 1941, Italy incorporated Kosovo and Çamëria into Albania.

During World War II the future of Kosovo became a major bone of contention between the two leading Albanian resistance groups, the communist-dominated National Liberation Movement and the non-communist National Front.[19] The National Front advocated the creation of an ethnic Albania after the war. The National Liberation Movement, which worked in close harmony with the Yugoslav partisans, had reluctantly agreed that Kosovo should be restored to Yugoslavia. In fact, at the request of Tito the Albanian communists had sent troops into Kosovo in late 1944 to disarm the population and to prepare the way for the resumption of Yugoslav control of that region.[20]

---

[19] *Dokumenta Kryesore të Partisë së Punës së Shqipërisë*, vol. I, ("Principal Documents of the Albanian Party of Labor") (hereafter cited as *Dokumenta Kryesore* I) (Tiranë: Instituti i Historisë së Partisë Pranë K.Q. të P.P. Sh., 1960), doc. 23, pp. 153–54; pp. 476–78, notes 57 and 62.

[20] Zavalani, *Histori e Shqipnis*, II, pp. 277–79; Sali Merkaj, "Faza e dytë e luftimeve të Ushtrisë Nacional-Çlirimtare për çlirimin e Kosovës dhe të Sanxhakut: nëndor-dhjetor 1944" ("The Second Phase of the Struggle of the Army of National Liberation for the Liberation of Kosovo and the Sanjak: No-

The Political System

When the Albanian people gained their independence in 1912, they had little experience in self-government. The ordinary Albanian, had never voted in an election. He had little knowledge of the structure and operation of the government. He also was so preoccupied with the problem of survival that he had little time to consider the problems facing the country.

Many Albanians apparently felt that independence would bring no great changes in the political life of the nation. The beys and the tribal chiefs expected to continue to govern their bailiwicks without any interference from the central authorities. Both the leaders of the Albanian national movement and the representatives of the Great Powers realized, however, that Albania could not achieve true national unity and protect herself against foreign intervention unless she possessed a strong effective central government. In the hope of creating a stable regime, the Conference of Ambassadors had offered the Albanian crown to Prince Wilhelm of Wied and had drawn up a moderately liberal constitution for the new state. Prince Wilhelm arrived in Albania in March, 1914, but left in September, 1914, shortly after the outbreak of World War I. During his six months on the throne the Prince had attempted to forge a unified Albanian state but had failed, owing to his own political inexperience, the intrigues of certain Albanian beys, and the constant interference of Austria, Italy, Greece, and Serbia in Albanian affairs. The Constitution of 1914—the first of seven under which the Albanian people lived be-

---

vember–December 1944"), *Studime Historike*, XX, No. 2 (1966), p. 11.

tween 1914 and 1944—became a dead letter with the departure of Wilhelm.

During World War I political activity in Albania was prohibited by the various Powers that occupied the country. After the conclusion of the Armistice, however, a group of Albanian patriots met at Durrës in December, 1918, and formed a provisional government under the presidency of Turhan Pasha. The Durrës government did not command much popular support. Many Albanians regarded it as little more than an Italian puppet regime. They were especially disappointed that Turhan Pasha and his cabinet did not take any positive steps to secure the withdrawal of the Italian army from Albania.

By January, 1920, the growing discontent with the Durrës government culminated in the convocation of the Congress of Lushnjë. The Congress framed a new constitution which placed executive power in the hands of a four-man regency, whose members were drawn from each of the major religious bodies in Albania. The major task confronting the Lushnjë government was to expel the Italian army. By August, 1920, this goal had been achieved.

Albanian political activity during the interwar period reached its zenith between 1921 and 1924.[21] It was mainly concentrated in the southern and central regions of the country and in the north Albanian city of Shkodër. The growing interest of the Albanian people in politics can be best illustrated by pointing out that

[21] For a general analysis of Albanian partisan politics during the early 1920s see Joseph S. Roucek, "Characteristics of Albanian Politics," *Social Science*, X (January, 1935), pp. 71–78; Stavro Skendi, *The Political Evolution of Albania, 1912–1944* (New York: Mid European Studies Center, 1954), pp. 5–8. For details see Swire, *Albania*, pp. 324–422 *passim*.; Pollo *et al.*, *Historia e Shqipërisë*, II, pp. 478–535.

eighty-six newspapers were established between 1921 and 1924.[22] Most of them expired after a few issues, but virtually all of them had been founded to propagate either liberal or conservative political ideas. In addition to the expansion of the Albanian press, this increasing political consciousness was also manifested by the attempts to form an Albanian agrarian party in 1922 and a socialist party in 1923.[23] Both of these movements ended in failure.

The principal issue in the Albanian political struggles of the early 1920s was whether Albania would continue to be governed by a coalition of landowners, ex-Ottoman bureaucrats, and tribal chieftans, led by Shevket Vërlaci and Ahmet Zogu, or whether political power would be transferred into the hands of Western-oriented liberals such as Fan Noli or Luigj Gurakuqi. The liberals argued that Albania could never become a modern state until the power of the old ruling class was broken, and a program of radical economic and social reforms instituted. Vërlaci and Zogu believed that no reforms should be attempted in Albania until law and order had been established in all parts of the

[22] T. Selenica, *Shqipria më 1927* ("Albania in 1927") (Tiranë: Shtypshkronja "Tirana," 1928), p. clxxiii.

[23] Bishop Noli believed that the first attempt to form an agrarian party in Albania occurred in 1922. Stefanaq Pollo, "Influenca e Revolucionit të Madh Socialist," p. 52, implies that agrarian political groups existed in Albania as early as 1919. For the abortive movement to form a socialist party in 1923, see Petro Lalaj, "Influenca e Revolucionit të Madh Socialist të Tetorit në Shqipëri, 1917–1924" ("The Influence of the Great October Socialist Revolution in Albania, 1917–1924"), *Buletin i Universitetit Shtetëror të Tiranës, Seria Shkencat Shoqërore,* XI, No. 2, (1957), pp. 28–29; and *Dokumenta mbi miqësine shqiptaro-sovjitike* ("Documents Concerning Albanian-Soviet Friendship") (Tiranë: Universiteti Shtetëror të Tiranës, 1957), p. 24, doc. 15 (hereafter cited as *Mbi miqësine shqiptaro-sovjetike*).

country. They also believed that if reforms were necessary, they should be introduced gradually, in order not to cause any internal upheavals.

The contest between the conservatives and the liberals reached its climax with the election of 1923, which, despite some government interference, was probably the most honest election ever held in Albania.[24] This election, however, was indecisive. The conservatives won forty of ninety-five seats in the Constituent Assembly; the liberals, thirty-five; and the remaining twenty were captured by independent candidates. When several independents threw their support to Zogu, he was able to remain in power. In February, 1924, after an unsuccessful attempt had been made upon his life, Zogu resigned as Prime Minister. His successor, Shevket Vërlaci, was unable to cope with the obstructionist tactics of the liberals in the Constituent Assembly and failed to resolve the serious economic problems plaguing the nation. The disaffected liberals and their allies organized an uprising against the government in late May.

The leader of the successful revolt, Fan Noli, was appointed Prime Minister on June 17, 1924. Noli, however, did not muster sufficient domestic or external support, and the coalition which had brought him to

[24] National Archives, Record Group 59, Department of State, *State Decimal File, 1910–1929*, 875.000/109. U. Grant Smith to Charles Evans Hughes, January 2, 1924 (hereafter cited as NA, *State Decimal File, 1910–1929*). Albanian communist historians maintain, however, that the Zog government used undue influence to manipulate the results of the election. See Selim Shpuza, *Revolucioni demokratiko-borgjez i qershorit 1924 në Shqipëri* ("The June 1924 Bourgeois-Democratic Revolution in Albania") (Tiranë: Ministria e Arësimit dhe Kulturës, 1959), pp. 15–16. The 1923 election was held to select delegates to a Constituent Assembly. This body also served as the Albanian Parliament between January and June, 1924.

power quickly fell apart. Britain and Yugoslavia were especially unsympathetic to his government and worked behind the scenes to prepare for Zogu's return in December, 1924.[25] After his return, as President, Zogu worked toward the transformation of Albania into a constitutional monarchy. Under the new constitution of 1928, as King Zog I, he was given broad authority. He used the power at his disposal to engineer the election of his supporters to Parliament, and having transformed the Parliament into a rubber-stamp body, he ruled as a dictator until 1939.[26]

In 1925, 1926, 1935, 1936, and 1937 antigovernment revolts broke out in Albania, but on each occasion Zog

[25] For an analysis of the factors which contributed to the downfall of the Noli regime see Swire, *Albania*, pp. 434–51; Shpuza, *Revolucioni demokratiko-borgjez*, pp. 27–39; Mentar Belegu, "Vendosja e regjimit feudoborgjez të A. Zogut—intervencioni i fuqive të huaja imperialiste" ("The Imposition of the Feudal-Bourgeois Regime of A. Zogu—The Intervention of the Foreign Imperialist Powers"), *Buletin i Universitetit Shtetëror të Tiranës, Seria Shkencat Shoqërore,* XI, No. 2 (1957), pp. 145–66; Arben Puto, "Çështja e njohjes ndërkombëtare të Qeverisë demokratike të 1924-s" ("The Question of the International Recognition of the 1924 Democratic Government"), *Studime Historike,* XVIII, No. 1 (1964), pp. 5–31; Hilmi Verteniku, "Politika e brendëshme e Qeverisë demokratike të 1924-ës ("The Internal Policy of the 1924 Democratic Government"), *Studime Historike,* XIX, No. 4 (1965), pp. 115–38. Noli expressed his own views concerning the overthrow of his regime in *La Fédération Balkanique,* II (April 30, 1925), pp. 256–57.

[26] There is no really adequate history in English of Albanian politics between 1925–39. Some insight into Albanian political life in the 1930's can be obtained from Joseph Swire, *King Zog's Albania* (London: Robert Hale and Company, 1937); Vandeleur Robinson, *Albania's Road to Freedom* (London: George Allen and Unwin, Ltd., 1941); Bernard Newman, *Albanian Backdoor* (London: Herbert Jenkins Limited, 1936). Two useful Albanian surveys are Pollo *et al., Historia e Shqipërisë,* II, pp. 558–681; and Zavalani, *Histori e Shqipnis,* II, pp. 186–219.

was able to crush them without too much difficulty. The army was loyal to him, and the majority of the Albanian people, who had again lost all interest in politics by the early 1930s, were not attracted to these movements. The only significant opposition to the regime came from disgruntled officials, students, intellectuals, workers, and a few businessmen who privately criticized Zog's policies. The anti-Zog forces, however, were sharply divided. Some were liberals in the Western tradition, others were communists or communist sympathizers, and a few were fascists. Furthermore, they had little contact with the peasant masses.

Zog did take some notice of discontent following the 1935 uprising when he appointed Mehdi Frashëri, a veteran liberal patriot, Prime Minister. The Frashëri cabinet, which was mainly comprised of young, educated liberals, remained in power for only one year. It was overthrown in November, 1936, when Zog found it necessary to surround himself with more pliant advisors as his relations with Italy became increasingly complex. His regime ended with the Italian invasion of April, 1939.

It was during the period between the two world wars that Albania was confronted with the task of transforming herself from a backward province of the Ottoman Empire into a modern national state. A strong, stable government capable of asserting its authority throughout the country and protecting the state against external threats had to be established. The economy had to be developed to the point at which Albania would not be wholly dependent on foreign assistance. The educational and cultural levels of the country had to be raised to levels commensurate with those of Western Europe.

It was obvious that the fledgling Albanian state

could not solve these problems alone. Outside assistance was necessary if the country was to survive. At the same time, however, the fierce nationalism of Albanians caused them to suspect the motives of any European state which sought to help them. Albania turned to the League of Nations for aid and, when the League refused this plea, to Italy. In the 1930s the Albanians realized the dangers that the Italian penetration posed to their independence and national sovereignty and sought to free themselves from Italian domination. By then it was too late. Albania had become too dependent upon Italy, and no other power was willing to assume Italy's burden in Albania. The Albanians were helpless and could not prevent Italy from engulfing their country in 1939.

After the surrender of Italy in September, 1943,[27] Germany restored Albania's independence. The Albanians then formed a new government whose executive power was vested in the hands of a four-man council of regents. The authority of this regime was challenged by the communists, who by this time controlled most of southern Albania and were advancing northward. At a conference held at Berat in October, 1944, the communist-dominated Anti-Fascist National Liberation Committee formed a provisional government under the leadership of Enver Hoxha. A month later the communists liberated Tiranë and assumed control in Albania.

The present-day Albanian communist leaders have

[27] The best published summary in English of developments in Albania between 1939–44 is Stavro Skendi, *The Political Evolution of Albania*, pp. 14–22. The best analysis currently available in English of the politics of this period is found in Amery, *Sons of the Eagle*. Two useful Albanian surveys are Pollo *et al.*, *Historia e Shqipërisë*, II, pp. 685–825; and Zavalani, *Histori e Shqipnis*, II, pp. 220–62.

not forgotten the difficulties which Albania experienced during the interwar period. When they seized power in 1944, they inherited virtually the same problems that had confronted their predecessors.

The Albanian Communist Movement 1917–41

Before 1917 few Albanians were acquainted with Marxist or socialist doctrines. Those who did have some knowledge of socialism were returned emigrants who had been exposed to this ideology while living abroad. In November, 1917, the Bolsheviks seized power in Russia and published the texts of the secret treaties, including the London Secret Treaty of 1915, which provided for the partition of Albania. Many Albanians were deeply moved by this gesture and some of them looked upon Lenin as the savior of their homeland.[28]

Few of those Albanians who were aware that the Bolsheviks had assumed control in Russia were able to comprehend the significance of the Bolshevik Revolution. Typical of the reaction of the average Albanian of the time was that of Sotir Vullkani, a young apprentice, who observed:

. . . to tell the truth, neither I nor my fellow apprentices really knew anything about the "Reds," but it warmed our hearts to hear that there (in Russia) the power of the wealthy had been broken and that the government was in

[28] Sotir Madhi, "V. I. Lenin dhe lëvizja çlirimtar e demokratike në Shqipëri" ("V. I. Lenin and the Democratic Liberation Movement in Albania"), *Rruga e Partisë* ("The Road of the Party"), VII (April 1960), pp. 10–15; Pollo, "Influenca e Revolucionit të Madh Socialist," *Historia ë Shqipërisë*, II, pp. 40–62; P. Lalaj, "Influenca e Revolucionit të Madh Socialist të Tetorit në Shqipëri, 1917–24," p. 16.

the hands of our comrades, the workers and the peasants. . . .[29]

Thus, insofar as the ordinary Albanian was concerned, the Bolsheviks were nothing more than reform-minded liberals in the Western sense of the term.

Other Albanians looked upon the Russian communists, with their slogans of national self-determination, as champions of the oppressed minorities of Europe. For this reason several prominent members of the United Committee of Kosovo and Çamëria (the Kosovo Committee), an organization dedicated to the restoration of these provinces to Albania, established regular contacts with Comintern agents in Yugoslavia early in 1920 after the Versailles Peace Conference had rejected the Albanian claims to these regions.[30] The Albanian nationalists were also encouraged by the propaganda of the newly created Balkan Communist Federation, which called for the readjustment of the frontiers of the Balkan states on the principle of national self-determination as a preliminary step to the establishment of a Balkan Federation of Socialist Republics. In December, 1921, Bajram Curri, one of the leaders of the Kosovo Committee, met with the Soviet minister in Vienna to discuss the Kosovo question. He presented the Russian diplomat with a memorandum which concluded:

The Albanian people await impatiently the determination of their frontiers not on the basis of brutal and bloody

[29] *Mbi miqësine shqiptaro-sovjetike*, p. 22, doc. 15.

[30] There were rumors as early as 1920 that the Kosovo Committee was being subsidized by the Comintern. See Swire, *Albania*, pp. 291–92; and Vladimir Gsovski and Kazmierz Grzybowski, *Government, Law and Courts in the Soviet Union and Eastern Europe* (London: Stevens and Sons Limited, 1959), I, p. 163.

historical considerations, but rather on the basis of the situation which actually exists today.

With the firm conviction that Soviet Russia will be able in the near future to determine the boundaries of Europe, especially in the Balkans, in a just manner, I pray that the great Soviet government will grant our just requests at that time.[31]

In addition to encouraging and later subsidizing the activities of the Kosovo Committee, the Comintern, acting through the Balkan Communist Federation, also sought to establish a communist party in Albania,[32] the only Balkan country lacking such an organization in the early 1920s. The communists also hoped to enlist the support of such liberal Albanian politicians as Bishop Fan Noli for their cause.[33]

The task of creating a communist party in Albania was entrusted to a young Albanian intellectual, Kostandin Boshnjaku,[34] who had been educated in Russia. In 1919 and 1920 Boshnjaku sought to infiltrate the liberal and nationalist political groups and to create pro-Soviet sentiment in Albania by attempting to convince the Albanian people that the Soviet Union had saved their homeland from partition by publishing the text of the Secret Treaty of London. Although Boshn-

[31] *Mbi miqësine shqiptaro-sovjetike*, p. 26, doc. 18.

[32] The need to organize an Albanian Communist Party was discussed at the Second Congress of the Balkan Communist Federation, which met in Vienna on February 24–28, 1921. Joseph Rothschild, *The Communist Party of Bulgaria, 1883–1936* (New York: Columbia University Press, 1959), pp. 227–28.

[33] Grigory Bessedovsky, *Revelations of a Soviet Diplomat*, trans. Matthew Norgate (London: Williams and Norgate, Ltd., 1931), p. 29.

[34] For an account of the career and activities of Boshnjaku, see NA, *State Decimal File, 1910–1929*, 875.000/B—, U. Grant Smith to Secretary of State Hughes, January 3, 1924; NA, *German Foreign Office Documents* (microfilm), T120, Roll 5026, L223883–5, von Kardorff to the Foreign Ministry, July 25, 1924.

jaku's propaganda did not have a great impact upon the Albanian masses, it did make a profound impression upon many young Albanian students and intellectuals, especially those who belonged to a social-political organization known as *Bashkimi* (The Union of Young Albanians), which had been formed in 1922.[35]

By 1923, when it became evident that Boshnjaku had failed, the Soviets adopted a new course of action. Between January and October, 1923, the Soviet government sought to establish diplomatic relations with Albania. In October of that year Moscow dispatched one of its most trusted agents in the Balkans, Dimitri Pentchev, to Tiranë to discuss this matter with Zogu.[36] At the same time Boshnjaku was ordered to abandon his efforts to create an Albanian Communist Party and to concentrate instead upon generating popular support for Albanian participation in the Balkan Communist Federation.

The Pentchev mission, however, was unsuccessful. Zogu refused to extend diplomatic recognition to the Soviet Union until the majority of the Great Powers had done so. He also rejected Pentchev's suggestion that a representative of the Soviet Red Cross be permitted to take up residence in Albania. Convinced that the main purpose of Pentchev's visit was to promote the communist cause in Albania, Zogu was determined not to give any encouragement to this movement,

[35] For the activities of *Bashkimi* see Pipi Mitrojorgji, *Histori e shkruar me gjak* ("History Written in Blood") (Tiranë; N. Sh. Botimeve "Naim Frashëri," 1961), pp. 10–19.

[36] For Soviet attempts to establish diplomatic relations with Albania during 1923, and for details of the Pentchev mission, see NA, *State Decimal File, 1910–1929*, 875.000/B–, U. Grant Smith to Secretary of State Hughes, January 3, 1924; NA, *German Foreign Office Documents* (microfilm), T120, Roll 5026, L223883–5, von Kardorff to the Foreign Ministry, 25 July 1924.

especially after the abortive communist attempt to seize power in Bulgaria in September, 1923.

Pentchev left Albania and Boshnjaku continued to direct all pro-communist activities in the country, taking an active role in the anti-Zogu coalition during the 1923 campaign. When the liberals failed to win a majority in these elections, the Comintern sent Pentchev to Albania to reassess the political situation. Pentchev and Boshnjaku were instrumental in bringing about a resolution to honor Lenin, who had recently died. The Albanian Constituent Assembly passed this tribute to the late Soviet dictator in February, 1924.[37]

Four months later, when the Albanian liberals seized power under the leadership of Fan Noli, the Executive Committee of the Comintern voted to support the new Albanian regime. The pro-communist elements in the Noli coalition were jubilant when a similar stand was taken by the Balkan Communist Federation and the Italian Communist Party. They urged Noli to establish diplomatic relations with the Soviet Union immediately, but Noli was reluctant to do so for fear of alienating the Great Powers.[38] In late June, Albania recognized the U.S.S.R. On September 4, Moscow reciprocated. A Soviet diplomatic mission arrived in Albania on December 16, but remained in the country only two days. Noli, under pressure from Britain and Yugoslavia, who feared the prospect of the Soviet Union using Albania as a base for military and propaganda activities in the Balkans, asked it to withdraw.[39]

[37] NA, *State Decimal File, 1910–1929*, 875.000/115, U. Grant Smith to Secretary of State Hughes, January 31, 1924; *ibid.*, 875.000/B/1, U. Grant Smith to Secretary of State Hughes, March 4, 1924; *ibid.*, 875.032/213, U. Grant Smith to Secretary of State Hughes, February 6, 1924.

[38] Interview with Bishop Fan Noli, July 8, 1960.

[39] Veli Dedi *et al.*, eds., *Dokumenta e materiale historike nga*

By the end of December, Zogu had regained control of the Albanian government and sent Noli along with his closest collaborators into exile. The triumph of Zogu dashed whatever opportunity there had existed for the creation of a strong communist movement in Albania during the 1920s. He moved quickly to crush the remaining liberal and pro-communist elements in Albania. In January, 1925, he ordered the dissolution of *Bashkimi* as a "revolutionary and Bolshevik organization." The Kosovo Committee was not permitted to function in Albania and the liberal press was silenced. A number of anti-Zogists, such as Bajram Curri and Zia Debra, were executed while scores of others were imprisoned.

Albanian exiles split up into several factions, the most important of which were the pro-communist *Komiteti Nacional Çlirimtar* (KONARE) (The National Liberation Committee) and the moderately liberal *Bashkimi Kombetar* (The National Union).[40] Of these two groups, KONARE was the more active and vocal in its opposition to Zogu. It attracted the more radical supporters of Fan Noli, and the deposed Prime Minister himself played an important role in its activities. This organization, based in Geneva, worked closely with the Balkan Communist Federation and received

---

lufta e popullit shqiptar për liri e demokraci 1917–1941 ("Documents and Historical Materials on the Struggle of the Albanian People for Freedom and Democracy 1917–1941") (Tiranë: Drejtoria e Arkivave Shtetërore të R.P. Sh., 1959) (hereafter cited as *Dokumenta e materiale historike, 1917–1941*), p. xi; *Mbi miqësine shqiptaro-sovjetike,* pp. 36–37, docs. 29–30.

[40] For an analysis of the Albanian exile groups in the late 1920s see NA, *State Decimal File, 1910–1929,* 875.000/233, Memorandum of Earl Brenner, "Present Conditions of Albanian Opposition Parties and Their Revolutionary Activities," September 21, 1927.

moral and financial assistance from that group. Its members published a newspaper and also wrote articles attacking the Zogu regime for *La Fédération Balkanique*. KONARE was also instrumental in making arrangements for some two dozen Albanians to go to the Soviet Union during the latter part of 1925 to receive ideological and political training.[41]

By 1928, owing primarily to financial difficulties, KONARE had fallen completely under communist domination, associated itself with the Comintern formally, and purged those members who had opposed this move. The organization then changed its name to *Çlirimi Nacional* (National Liberation).[42] In August, 1928, the Albanian communists in the Soviet Union established an Albanian Communist Party in exile. This group was composed of the most promising of the Albanian political refugees who had been studying and working in the U.S.S.R. since 1925. Its primary function was to prepare organizers and propagandists for service in Albania, where several communist cells had been clandestinely established in 1927.[43]

In 1929, the Comintern ordered several agents to

[41] Shpuza, *Revolucioni demokratiko-borgjez*, pp. 47–48; Koço Tashko, "Ali Kelmendi—militant i shquar i lëvizjes komuniste shqiptare" ("Ali Kelmendi—Distinguished Militant of the Albanian Communist Movement"), *Rruga e Partisë*, VII (May, 1960), pp. 20–21.

[42] *Dokumenta Kryesore* I, pp. 12–13, doc. 1; Tashko, "Ali Kelmendi—militant i shquar," p. 21; Vangjel Moisiu, *Lufta për krijimin e Partisë Komuniste të Shqipërisë, 1917–1941* ("The Struggle for the Creation of the Albanian Communist Party, 1917–41") (Tiranë: Instituti i Historisë së Partisë Pranë K.Q. të P.P. Sh., 1957), p. 38.

[43] Sotir Manushi, ed., *Ali Kelmendi, militant i shquar i lëvizjes komuniste shqiptare* ("Ali Kelmendi, Distinguished Militant of the Albanian Communist Movement") (Tiranë: Instituti i Historisë së Partisë Pranë K.Q. P.P.Sh., 1960), pp. 3–6; Tashko, "Ali Kelmendi—militant i shquar" pp. 23–24.

Albania, to organize a full-fledged communist party there. Ali Kelmendi, a former member of *Bashkimi* and a staunch backer of Fan Noli during the 1924 revolution, was entrusted with this responsibility. In the spring of 1930 he arrived in Kosovo; he hoped to establish a number of communist cells in the Albanian settlements of that region but met with little success.

The Albanian communist movement suffered another blow when Bishop Fan Noli, wearied and disillusioned by his life as a political exile, announced in 1930 his retirement from politics and his plan to return to the United States to resume his duties as spiritual leader of the Albanian Orthodox Church in America.[44]

Undaunted by his experiences in Kosovo and by the withdrawal of Bishop Noli from the communist movement, Ali Kelmendi crossed the border into Albania and resolutely strove to unite there the various communist and pro-communist factions. He soon realized that this task was far more difficult than either he or the Comintern had imagined. Although there was a great deal of opposition to the policies of King Zog and to the ever-growing Italian influence in the country, the Albanians had little sympathy for and even less understanding of communist ideas.

Despite these handicaps Kelmendi did manage to establish several communist groups in Albania between 1930 and 1932. The most important of these was *Puna* (Work) of Korçë, whose membership was largely recruited from the communist cells which had been formed in 1927–28. Other communist groups

[44] Fan S. Noli, ed., *Fiftieth Anniversary Book of the Albanian Orthodox Church in America* (Boston: Albanian Orthodox Church in America, 1960), p. 127; Glenn A. McLain, *Albanian Exposé* (Quincy, Massachusetts: Premier Press, 1952), pp. 10–11.

were organized in Vlorë, Elbasan, and Krujë. Their combined membership was about thirty and their main activity was to infiltrate the few labor organizations then in existence in Albania.[45]

In March, 1932, Kelmendi went to Moscow to give an accounting to the Comintern of his activities in Albania and to receive new instructions. When he returned to Albania in the late spring of 1932 he was arrested and remained in custody until November 17, 1935.[46]

When Kelmendi was imprisoned, the Albanian communists found themselves without a strong leader, and began to quarrel among themselves. Nevertheless, the communist movement in Albania managed to survive and to grow. In 1933 the Korçë communist group formed a labor organization which also took the name *Puna*. Later other groups were organized for tailors, shoemakers, and clerks. By 1935 a second branch of *Puna* was established among the workers in the oil fields at Kuçovë. During the 1930s these organizations called periodic strikes and demonstrations which sought to call public attention to the economic grievances of the workers and the growing stranglehold on the economy of Albania by Italian interests. The most important of these communist-inspired public protests were the strikes of the Kuçovë oil workers in November, 1935, and February, 1936, and the so-called Korçë bread riot of 1936. Several communists also participated in the short-lived Fieri uprising against the Zog regime in August, 1935.[47] Quick and resolute action on

[45] See reports of Ali Kelmendi to the Comintern for 5 and 7 March 1932 in Manushi, "Ali Kelmendi—militant i shquar," pp. 22–27.

[46] *Ibid.*, pp. 7–8.

[47] *Ibid.*, 8–15; Ndreçi Plasari, "Mbi themelimin e Partisë Komuniste Shqiptare" ("Concerning the Founding of the Al-

the part of the Albanian government on each of these occasions prevented these incidents from getting out of hand.

Intellectuals and students had traditionally been in the vanguard of the Albanian liberal movements, and in the 1930s they were among the most steadfast opponents of the domestic and foreign policies of King Zog. While only a handful of intellectuals, laborers, and students actually became members of the communist cells which began to spring up in various parts of Albania in the 1930s, many others publicly applauded and supported the communists and other anti-Zogist groups in their efforts to bring about sweeping reforms in virtually every phase of Albanian life.[48]

The communists sought to influence the educated and socially conscious Albanians by writing articles for such liberally oriented journals as *A.B.C.* and *Relindja* ("Rebirth"), which appeared in the mid 1930s. Between April, 1936, and February, 1937, the members of the Korçë communist group were prominently in-

banian Communist Party"), *Buletin për Shkencat Shoqërore*, X, No. 4 (1956), pp. 9–10.

[48] For a summary and evaluation of the role of the Albanian intellectuals in the communist movement, see Vehbi Bala, "Çështje të historisë së letërsisë shqipe: Rreth realizimit tonë kritik në *Bota e Re* të Korçës" ("The Problem of the History of Albanian Literature: Concerning Our Critical Realism in *The New World* of Korçë"), *Buletin, për Shkencat Shoqërore*, X, No. 3 (1956), pp. 136–172 *passim.*; "Revista *Bota e Re* e Korçës" ("The Review *The New World* of Korçë"), *Nëndori*, III (May 1956), pp. 118–23; Viron Koka, "Lufta ideologjike e revistës *Bota e Re* kundër reaksionit zogist (1936–1937)" ("The Ideological Struggle of the Review *The New World* Against the Zogist Reaction, 1936–1937"), *Studime Historike*, XVIII, No. 2 (1964), pp. 121–45, "Problemi i unitetit kombëtar në lëvizjen ideologjike të viteve 30 të shekullit XX" "The Problem of National Unity in the Ideological Movement of the 1930s"), *Studime Historike*, XIX, No. 2 (1965), pp. 69–80.

volved in the publication of a bi-monthly review, *Bota e Re* ("The New World"), which at the height of its popularity enjoyed a circulation of 3,000, a figure greater than that of any other journal appearing at this period. *Bota e Re* devoted much of its space to discussions of social and economic problems. It also printed short stories by such communist or pro-communist Albanian writers as Sterjo Spasse, Dhimitër S. Shuteriqi, Aleks Çaçi, Shevket Musaraj, Millosh Gjergj Nikolla (Migjeni), as well as others whose work was highly critical of conditions in Albania. In February, 1937, the Albanian authorities forced *Bota e Re* to cease publication when they began to fear its impact upon the people.[49]

Albanian communists also began to smuggle translations of Marxist-Leninist tracts and the works of such well-known Soviet writers as Maxim Gorky into Albania for distribution among students and intellectuals. The influx of this communist literature had reached such alarming proportions by 1937 that the Albanian government felt impelled to pass a series of laws regulating the importation of books, newspapers, and periodicals.[50]

Thus during the mid- and late-1930s, the Albanian communists concentrated their efforts on spreading communist propaganda in the hope of capitalizing on the unrest which existed in the country, but made little progress toward creating a unified Albanian Communist Party. When Ali Kelmendi was released from prison in November, 1935, he found the communists hopelessly divided, although they were numerically

[49] See "Revista *Bota e Re* e Korçës."
[50] *Fletorja Zyrtare* (Tiranë) ("The Official Gazette"), February 5, 1937; March 19, 1937; April 1, 1937; April 21, 1937; April 22, 1937.

stronger than ever before. Immédiately, he went to Greece and then to Turkey to meet with agents of the Comintern to secure their permission to purge certain unorthodox elements from the Albanian communist movement. Unable to obtain official approval for this purge, he returned to Albania where once again he was arrested and, in September, 1936, deported.[51]

Kelmendi made his way to Paris where he contacted the leaders of the Albanian communist group there. In December, 1936, Kelmendi, Koço Tashko, and Halim Xhelo were called to Moscow to receive new instructions concerning the strategy and tactics to be employed by the Albanian communists in light of the decisions of the Seventh Congress of the Comintern, which had met during July and August, 1935. Once more the Comintern expressed the view that conditions were not yet right for the creation of a communist party in Albania. Instead the Albanian communists were ordered to reorganize their cells, strengthen their ties with the masses, co-operate with those organizations seeking to obtain "democratic rights" for the Albanian people, and promote pacificism in Albania. Koço Tashko was then dispatched to Albania to convey these directives to the Albanian communists.[52]

When Tashko arrived in Albania in early 1937, he found there four major communist groups. The first

---

[51] *Dokumenta e materiale historike 1917–1941*, p. 376, doc. 424.

[52] Tashko, "Ali Kelmendi—militant i shquar," p. 23. The Comintern had instructed Kelmendi and Tashko and "several other comrades" to return to Albania "by legal means." Tashko received permission from the Albanian authorities to re-enter the country, but Kelmendi did not. He remained in France from 1937 until his death in February, 1939. For the activities of Kelmendi in France between 1937–39, see Manushi, "Ali Kelmendi, militant i shquar," pp. 6–18, 41–53.

and most important of these was the Korçë group, which maintained branches in Durrës and Tiranë. Among the more prominent leaders of this faction were Koçi Xoxe, a tinsmith, and Enver Hoxha, a school teacher. The Korçë group was the oldest and most active of the communist organizations in Albania, and its members generally supported the new Comintern line. Its greatest weakness was its failure to develop strong ties with the masses. Next in importance was the Shkodër group, which had been founded in 1936 but did not become fully organized until 1938. The leader of this faction was a young intellectual, Zef Mala. Among the other notable members of this group were Vasil Shanto, a baker; Tuk Jakova, a carpenter; Liri Gega, an intellectual; and Qemal Stafa, a student. The Shkodër group, which concentrated most of its efforts on building up the strength of its cadres during the late 1930s, also had limited ties with the working class. Neither of the two remaining factions, the Tiranë group headed by Aristidh Qendro and the *Zjarri* (Fire) organization under the leadership of Andrea Zisi, was considered to be an orthodox communist group. The former was comprised mainly of dissidents from the Korçë group, while the latter, which had been originally formed by Albanian students studying in Greece, maintained an outlook which closely paralleled that of the Greek archeomarxists.[53]

When Tashko realized that he could not secure unqualified endorsement of the Comintern policies from

[53] For an analysis of the status of the Albanian Communist movement in the 1930s see Moisiu, *Lufta për krijimin*, pp. 39–60; *Dokumenta Kryesore* I, p. 467, n. 7; p. 468, nn. 9, 10; p. 470, n. 14; Vladimir Dedijer, *Marredhanjet jugosllavo-shqiptare, 1939–48* ("Yugoslav-Albanian Relations, 1939–48") (Beograd: Prosveta, 1949), pp. 9–14.

the various Albanian communist factions, he associated himself with the Korçë group. Between 1937 and 1939 each of the Albanian communist organizations operated independently of the others. The Korçë and Shkodër groups each published journals designed to acquaint their readers with the basic tenets of communist ideology and also distributed communist tracts and pamphlets to students, intellectuals, and interested workers.[54] In January, 1939, the Albanian government sought to put an end to this activity by arresting seventy-three individuals for disseminating communist propaganda. Brought to trial in early February, fifty-one of the accused were found guilty and received sentences ranging from one month to ten years imprisonment. Among those convicted were Zef Mala, Vasil Shanto, Emin Duraku, Qemal Stafa, and Pandi Kristo. A large number of those who had been tried were members of the Shkodër group and several of them publicly confessed that they were communists.[55]

When Italy invaded Albania on April 7, 1939, the communists were too divided to organize an effective resistance movement. As had been the case throughout the 1930s, their main weakness was the absence of a strong central organization capable of uniting the warring factions and of commanding the respect of the masses. In the hope of remedying this situation, the Korçë and Shkodër groups established a joint central committee in October, 1939, and in the spring of 1940, a "committee of arbitration," comprised of representatives from most of the Albanian communist factions. Both of these measures failed. Instead of uniting the

[54] See *Dokumenta e materiale historike 1917–1941*, pp. 383–423, *passim.*, docs. 435–497.

[55] Moisiu, *Lufta për krijimin*, p. 52; *Dokumenta Kryesore* I, p. 472, n. 29.

communists, new rivalries and personal feuds resulted in the formation of several new factions, including the *Të Rinjve* ("The Youth Group"), which was another offshoot of the Korçë group. By early 1941 there were eight communist organizations, two of them Trotsky-ite, operating in Albania.[56]

At this juncture the Yugoslav Communist Party (YCP) intervened to help unify the Albanian Communist movement. According to Vladimir Dedijer, the Yugoslav communists had first sought to use their influence to end the strife among the Albanian communists during the summer of 1939, when they had instructed Miladin Popović, secretary of the Regional Committee for Kosovo-Metohija (Kosmet), to contact the leaders of the Shkodër group to ascertain what steps could then be taken to create an Albanian Communist Party.[57] On this occasion, however, Popović met with little success in his endeavors. At the Fifth Congress of the YCP, which was held in the summer of 1940, he delivered a report concerning the status of the Albanian communist movement. In order to encourage the Albanian communists to take more resolute action against the Italians, this Congress reaffirmed the stand of the YCP, first taken in 1928, that Kosovo should be restored to Albania.[58] The Yugoslav communists further decided to detach the Kosmet Regional Commit-

---

[56] Ndreçi Plasari, *Krijimi i Partisë Komuniste të Shqipërisë, 1939–1941* ("The Creation of the Albanian Communist Party, 1939–1941") (Tiranë: Instituti i Historisë së Partisë Pranë K.Q. të P.P. Sh., 1958), p. 25. See *Dokumenta Kryesore* I, p. 14, doc. 1; Moisiu, *Lufta për krijimin*, p. 53. Dedijer, *Marredhanjet jugosllavo-shqiptare*, p. 15.

[57] *Ibid.*, pp. 10–11.

[58] "Die albanische Minderheit in Jugoslawien," *Wissenschaftlicher Dienst Südosteuropa*, VI (Sept.–Oct. 1957), p. 164.

tee from the Montenegrin Provincial Committee and to place it under the direct jurisdiction of the Central Committee of the YCP. The Kosmet Regional Committee was to take immediate steps to assist the Albanians in building up an effective resistance organization as a preliminary step toward creating an Albanian Communist Party.[59] Owing to unsettled conditions in Yugoslavia following the Nazi invasion and the imprisonment of Popović, the Kosmet Committee made no overt attempt to cement its relations with the Albanian communists until September, 1941, when it dispatched Dušan Mugoša, a member of the Central Committee, to Albania.

Mugoša's mission to Albania was prompted by a request from the Shkodër group for aid in forming an Albanian Communist Party. The Korçë group boycotted Mugoša when he could not prove to their satisfaction that he was a bona fide member of the Yugoslav Communist Party. After Mugoša returned to Yugoslavia a delegation from the Korçë group contacted him. They apologized for their conduct in Tiranë and expressed their willingness to participate in the movement to form an Albanian Communist Party. In October, 1941, Mugoša returned to Albania and with the help of the Albanian communists succeeded in liberating Popović, who had been captured by the Nazis.[60]

During the last weeks of October, Mugoša and Popović conferred with the leaders of each of the Albanian communist factions. After much wrangling the Korçë, Shkodër, and Youth groups agreed to put their

[59] Harry Hamm, *Albania—China's Beachhead in Europe*, trans. Victor Anderson (New York: Frederick A. Praeger, 1963), pp. 84–85.

[60] Dedijer, *Marredhanjet jugosllavo-shqiptare*, pp. 12–17.

differences aside and to unite to form an Albanian Communist Party. On November 4, 1941, twenty delegates representing each of the three participating factions met with Mugoša and Popović in Tiranë. After five days of heated discussion, agreement was finally reached concerning organizational and policy matters.[61] A provisional Central Committee was then chosen, and Enver Hoxha was elected secretary of this body.[62] The Central Committee then framed a resolution which discussed the history, errors, and successes of the Albanian communist movement. It also contained a twenty-three-point program to guide the Party in its activities. The Central Committee also issued a manifesto calling upon the Albanian people to resist the Axis aggressors by every possible means.[63] Shortly after

[61] *Ibid.*, pp. 17–18; *Dokumenta Kryesore* I, pp. 7–8; Moisiu, *Lufta për krijimin*, pp. 28–31; Ndreçi Plasari, *Partia Komuniste e Shqipërisë—organizatore e fitores historike të popullit shqiptar në Luftën Nacional-Çlirimtare kundër pushtuesve fashistë dhe tradhëtarëve* ("The Albanian Communist Party—Organizer of the Historic Victory of the Albanian People in the War of National Liberation Against the Fascist Occupiers and Traitors") (Tiranë: Instituti i Historisë së Partisë Pranë KQ të PPSH, 1964), pp. 33–60 *passim*. The Albanian sources make no mention of the role played by the Yugoslavs in unifying the Albanian communist movement. The validity of the Yugoslav accounts, however, has been verified by the fact that the notes which Popović kept during October and November, 1941, were captured by the Albanian authorities, along with other documents, in a raid in early 1943. They were subsequently used as evidence in a trial of suspected communists held in Tiranë in May, 1943. Dedijer, *Marredhanjet jugosllavo-shqiptare*, p. 16; Stavro Skendi, "Albania Within the Slav Orbit: Advent to Power of the Communist Party," *Political Science Quarterly*, LXIII (June 1948), n. p. 260.

[62] Dedijer, *Marredhanjet jugosllavo-shqiptare*, p. 18. Enver Hoxha is the only one of the original Central Committee of the Albanian Communist Party who is currently a member of the Central Committee.

[63] *Dokumenta Kryesore* I, pp. 9–28, docs. 1 and 2.

the November meeting, 130 persons were admitted into the ranks of the Party.[64]

The Albanian Communist Party (Partia Komuniste e Shqipërisë) had thus been finally established after a struggle of almost twenty years. While it is true that it required a world war, foreign occupation, and Yugoslav assistance to achieve this goal, it should also be noted that the objective could not have been realized without the existence of a small, hard-core, native communist movement.

[64] Mihal Bisha, "Nga historia e ndërtimit të Partisë ("From the History of the Establishment of the Party"), *Rruga e Partisë*, VI (November 1959), p. 88.

2: THE ENTRY OF ALBANIA INTO THE COMMUNIST PARTY STATE SYSTEM

The Communist Seizure of Power in Albania, 1941–44

The most important tasks which confronted the Albanian Communist Party after its formation were to recruit new members, to strengthen its ties with the masses, and to gain control of and unify the Albanian resistance movement. Since many of the leaders of the Albanian communist movement were relatively young, and since the youth of Albania had traditionally played an important role in the Albanian liberal and revolutionary movements, the Party decided to create a communist youth group. On November 23, 1941, the Albanian Communist Youth Organization was established in Tiranë. Two members of the Central Committee of the Albanian Communist Party, Qemal Stafa and Nako Spiru, were elected to the Central Committee of the Youth Organization to ensure communist dominance of this group. By early 1942, branches of this organization had been founded in the major towns of Albania.[1] In this manner, several thousand young people in Albania were drawn into the communist movement during the course of World War II.

---

[1] Mitrojorgji, *Histori e Shkruar me Gjak*, pp. 69–83.

Next the Party launched an extensive propaganda campaign to popularize the communist resistance movement and to raise the funds necessary to finance its operations.[2] It also dispatched cadres into the various regions of the country to reorganize the guerrilla bands which had been in operation since the early days of the Italian invasion, and to form new units in those areas where there were none. By the summer of 1942, the communist-dominated resistance forces had grown in strength to the point where they were able to harass the Italian occupation forces with increasing regularity and effectiveness.[3]

While the Albanian communists were fairly successful in arousing active opposition to the Italian army and the Albanian collaborationist regime, they were far less successful in attracting wide-scale popular support for their movement. For this reason the Central Committee of the Party ordered its agents in the field to de-emphasize their pro-communist propaganda and instead to concentrate upon forming "national liberation councils" which would include "anti-fascists of all political factions."[4]

Another major source of weakness within the Albanian communist movement at this time was the lack of doctrinal purity. This problem was brought to light at the Consultative Meeting of the Albanian Communist Party, which was held in Tiranë between April

[2] *Dokumenta Kryesore* I, pp. 30–31, doc. 4.

[3] Shefqet Peçi, *Kujtime dhe Dokumenta nga Lufta Nacional Çlirimtare* ("Reminiscences and Documents from the War of National Liberation"), 2 vols. (Tiranë: N. Sh. Botimeve "Naim Frashëri," 1959, 1961), I, pp. 13–24; II, pp. 19–45.

[4] *Dokumenta Kryesore* I, pp. 48–49, doc. 8. The national liberation councils were similar to those which were organized under communist leadership in Greece and Yugoslavia during the early days of the war.

8 and 10, 1942. The meeting specifically scored the policies of the *Zjarri* faction, which had refused to co-operate with the Albanian Communist Party and had been urging the Albanian people to refrain from taking up arms until Italy had been brought to her knees by the Allied Powers.[5]

The delegates also discussed and condemned the "anti-Party stand" of the *Të Rinjve* (Youth) faction. Under the leadership of Sadik Premte and Anastas Lulo the *Të Rinjve* had opposed the Party's attempt to broaden its base by recruiting peasants into the communist movement and had also insisted that the Party should concentrate upon strengthening its cadres rather than engaging in guerrilla warfare. The leaders of this group were further accused of attempting to sabotage the Communist Youth Organization and of spreading anti-Soviet propaganda.[6]

The leadership of the Albanian Communist Party, however, was reluctant to purge the dissident members of the *Të Rinjve* group at this time, fearing that such a step might further weaken the Party. This course of action did not meet with the approval of the Yugoslav advisers to the Albanian Communist Party. After several months of prodding by the Yugoslavs, an extraordinary Party Conference was convened in Tiranë during the last week of June, 1942, to deal with the problem of the *Të Rinjve* faction. At this meeting,

[5] *Ibid.*, pp. 58–59, 64, doc. 9; Plasari, *Partia Komuniste e Shqipërisë 1941–1944*, pp. 74–82.

[6] Jorgji Sota, *Partia Komuniste Shqiptare në luftë për çlirimin e vendit dhe për vendosjen e pushtetit popullor, nëndor 1941– nëndor 1944* ("The Albanian Communist Party in the Struggle for the Liberation of the Country and for the Establishment of the People's Power, November 1941–November 1944") (Tiranë: [Instituti i Historisë së Partisë Pranë K.Q.P.P. Sh.] 1957), pp. 10–14.

Lulo, Premte, and five other leaders of the anti-Party group were expelled from the Party "for an indefinite period."[7]

Once the threat posed by the *Të Rinjve* faction had been eliminated, the Central Committee of the Albanian Communist Party decided to launch a series of well-coordinated raids upon Italian supply and communication lines in late July 1942. Shortly after this operation was underway, the communists realized that they would have to take steps to keep the Albanian resistance movement under their control. The Party decided that it was time to implement its program for the creation of a united front of all anti-facist forces in Albania.[8]

On September 16, 1942, at the invitation of the Albanian Communist Party, the leaders of the resistance groups then operating in Albania met at the village of Pezë near Tiranë. The delegates who attended this meeting agreed to form a united front organization, which was called the *Levizja Nacional Çlirimtar* (The National Liberation Movement—NLM). A Central Committee of ten members, which included both communists and non-communists, was elected to direct the activities of this group. The delegates agreed to wage a struggle "to the end" against the Axis and its Albanian collaborationists, to unite the Albanian people "irrespective of their religion, region, or political views into a single anti-fascist national liberation front," and to "organize national liberation councils in all parts of Albania." It is now clear that the communists fully expected to dominate this organization and that they hoped to use it as a front

[7] *Dokumenta Kryesore* I, pp. 77, 81–84, doc. 11; Dedijer, *Marredhanjet jugosllavo-shqiptare*, pp. 106–7.

[8] Sota, *Partia Komuniste*, pp. 16–20.

to seize power once the Axis had been driven from Albania.[9]

Not all Albanians, however, were deceived by this stratagem. In the latter part of October, 1942, a group of moderately liberal Albanians led by the respected patriot, Midhat Frashëri, and a veteran politician, Ali Klissura, formed a rival group which was known as the *Balli Kombëtar* (BK—The National Front). This faction favored the establishment of a republican government after the war, the inauguration of a program of economic and social reform, and the preservation of the ethnic Albanian state as created by the fascists in 1941. The founders of the BK felt that, unless an alternative program and party existed in Albania, the country would fall to the communists by default.[10] The BK and the communist-dominated NLM thus became the principal contenders in the power struggle which gripped Albania between the autumn of 1942 and the autumn of 1944. In many respects the contest between the BK and the NLM followed a course similar to that which took place between Tito's Partisans and Mihailović's Chetniks. Indeed the communist victory in Yugoslavia was a vital factor in the communist triumph in Albania.

The Albanian communists were naturally alarmed by the formation of the BK. Before launching a campaign against the BK, they received in December, 1942, permission from the Comintern to call a National Party Conference to purge their ranks of all disloyal elements. The Comintern instructed the Albanian

[9] *Ibid.*, pp. 20–24; Mahmut Çungu, "One Hundred Days Inside Albania" (unpublished MS, Istanbul, 1943), pp. 9–13.

[10] Skendi, *Albania*, p. 20; Çungu, "One Hundred Days," pp. 13–14; Sota, *Partia Komuniste*, pp. 26–27; Plasari, *Partia Komuniste e Shqipërisë 1941–1944*, pp. 99–104.

Party to intensify its resistance activities through the NLM, to broaden the leadership of the NLM including "as great a number as possible of honest nationalists and patriotic Albanians," to strengthen its own ties with the peasantry, and to expel those individuals whose views did not conform to the party line.[11]

The First National Conference of the Albanian Communist Party was convened on March 17, 1943. There were some 70 delegates in attendance, representing approximately 700 members of the Albanian Communist Party. After voicing its approval of the Comintern directives, the Conference voted to form an Army of National Liberation, which, it was hoped, would encompass all of those groups that were actively engaged in fighting the Axis forces in Albania. The Party also resolved to strengthen its ties with the masses by initiating a propaganda campaign to convince the Albanian people that the Party sought to free them from tyranny and to improve their standard of living. Sadik Premte and Anastas Lulo were again condemned, and the Party resolved to continue its efforts to eradicate all ideological heresies within its ranks. A permanent Central Committee of eleven members and six candidates was chosen, and Enver Hoxha was re-elected First Secretary of this body.[12]

[11] Sota, *Partia Komuniste*, pp. 31–32; *Dokumenta Kryesore* I, p. 93.

[12] For accounts of the First National Conference of the Albanian Communist Party, see Sota, *Partia Komuniste*, pp. 32–38; *Dokumenta Kryesore* I, pp. 95–118, doc. 14; Plasari, *Partia Komuniste e Shqipërisë 1941–1944*, pp. 119–32; The attitude and policies of the Albanian communists toward Sadik Premte and Anastas Lulo are discussed in Sota, *Partia Komuniste*, pp. 38–41 and *Dokumenta Kryesore* I, pp. 136–46, doc. 19. Lulo was captured and executed by the Albanian communists in 1943, but Premte managed to elude capture and fled from Albania at the end of the war.

Following the Congress, the Albanian communists worked to consolidate their position within the NLM. At the suggestion of the communists, a General Staff of the Army of National Liberation was established on July 10, 1943. Enver Hoxha was named political commissar of this group. Two weeks later, when the Albanian Army of National Liberation was established, another communist, Sipro Moisiu, was appointed commander-in-chief.[13] In this manner, the Albanian communists obtained effective control over the majority of the guerrilla bands which were operating in the country by 1943.

During the summer of 1943, some of the more patriotic and responsible members of the BK and the NLM made a determined effort to bring about a union between these two groups. They were aided in their endeavors by the launching of the Allied invasion of Sicily, which raised the possibility of an Allied landing in Albania.[14] Finally, the pressures exerted on both contending factions by the British Military Mission, which had arrived in Albania in the spring of 1943, helped bring them together.

On August 2, 1943, representatives of the BK and NLM met at the village of Mukaj. Here, after a great deal of bickering, they agreed to form the Committee for the Salvation of Albania. This Committee, which was composed of an equal number of members from both factions, was charged with the tasks of directing

[13] Peçi, *Kujtime dhe Dokumenta*, I, pp. 55–56. Stiliano Sallabanda, ed., *Kronikë e Ditëve të Stuhishme* ("Chronicle of Tempestuous Days") (Tiranë: Degë së Historisë Ushtarake të MMP, 1962), pp. 210–11.

[14] Skendi, *Albania*, p. 21; Sota, *Partia Komuniste*, pp. 49–50; *Dokumenta Kryesore* I, p. 476, n. 57. The communist sources insist that the overtures for cooperation between the BK and the NLM came solely from the latter group.

the war effort and administering those areas which had been liberated from the Axis. The major stumbling block to the conclusion of this agreement was the insistence of the BK that Kosovo-Metohija be included in the frontiers of the Albanian state. Both sides, however, finally agreed to a compromise proposal that the future of this region should be determined by a postwar plebescite.[15]

When the NLM delegates returned to their headquarters, the leadership of that organization and the Communist Party, including Enver Hoxha, approved the formation of a genuine united front as envisioned by the Mukaj Agreement. They also seemed favorably disposed to the stipulation that a plebiscite be held in Kosovo-Metohija at the conclusion of the war. At this point, the senior Yugoslav representative then present in Albania, Svetozar Vukmanović-Tempo, denounced the agreement and ordered the Albanian communists and the NLM to repudiate it at once.[16] The Albanian communists immediately reversed their stand and dispatched a circular letter on August 8, 1943, to all local party organizations in the country. In this communication, the communists were instructed to repudiate the Mukaj Agreement, end all collaboration with the BK, and intensify their ideological and organizational activity.[17] There was no longer any doubt that the Al-

[15] Sota, *Partia Komuniste*, pp. 50–52; *Dokumenta Kryesore* I, pp. 476–77, n. 57.

[16] The communist Albanian sources dealing with the Mukaj Conference and its aftermath maintain that the Albanian communists took the initiative in denouncing the Mukaj Agreement. See, *inter alia*, Plasari, *Partia Komuniste e Shqipërisë 1941–1944*, pp. 154–59. The Yugoslav accounts, however, insist that the Albanians were pressured into taking this step. For a summary of the Yugoslav version of these events see Dedijer, *Marredhanjet jugosllavo-shqiptare*, pp. 94–95.

[17] *Dokumenta Kryesore* I, pp. 153–54, doc. 23.

banian Communist Party was under the complete domination of the Yugoslavs.

The repudiation of the Mukaj Agreement by the communists, coupled with the German occupation of Albania following the overthrow of the Italian fascist regime in September 1943, set the stage for the final phase of the struggle between the communist and non-communist forces for control of Albania.

On September 1, 1943, under the watchful eyes of a Yugoslav delegation, the second conference of the Albanian National Liberation Movement met at Labinot. After formally denouncing the Mukaj Agreement, the delegates agreed to launch a full scale campaign to liberate Albania, to destroy the influence of the BK, and to form national liberation councils in those parts of the country that had been evacuated by the Italian army in order to prevent the BK or other non-communist elements from assuming power there. A General National Liberation Council was then appointed to supervise the work of the local units. By the end of September, 1943, in accordance with the instructions of the Conference and subsequent Party directives, the NLM unleashed a concerted military and propaganda offensive against both the BK and the Germans, who had by now rushed some two and a half divisions into Albania.[18]

The Germans assumed control of Albania in September, 1943, and sought to win the support of the people by granting Albania a large degree of self-government. A number of prominent members of the BK and many genuinely patriotic Albanians such as the former liberal Prime Minister Mehdi Frashëri agreed to serve in the German-sponsored regime, because they

[18] Sota, *Partia Komuniste*, pp. 53–55. *Dokumenta Kryesore* I, pp. 156–69, docs. 24, 25.

feared that the resistance to the Germans and the civil war between the BK and the NLM might weaken Albania by bloodshed, so that she would be an easy prey for her greedy neighbors after the war. These Albanian politicians also viewed with growing concern the increasing communist influence in the country. They realized long before it became evident to the average Albanian that the NLM was nothing more than a communist front designed to camouflage the Party's ultimate objective—the seizure of power in Albania.[19]

During the autumn of 1943 the communists solidified their grip on the NLM when Abas Kupi, one of the last important non-communist figures in that group, broke with the organization after its disavowal of the Mukaj Agreement. Kupi, a Geg tribal chieftain and a loyal supporter of King Zog, had been smuggled into Albania by the British in early 1941 to help to organize guerrilla bands in northern Albania. He had been one of the founders of the NLM in 1942 and was a member of the General Council of National Liberation at the time of his defection. In late November, 1943, he established the Legality organization, which derived most of its support from the Northern Albanian tribesmen who favored the restoration of the monarchy.[20]

Thus, by the end of 1943, the opposition to the communist-dominated NLM was divided into three groups. These were the German-sponsored Albanian govern-

[19] Mehdi Frashëri, *Nacionalizma shqipëtare dhe faktorët ngatrestarë të brendëshmë dhe jashtmë* ("Albanian Nationalism and Troublesome Internal and External Factors") (Tiranë: n.p., 1943), pp. 20–24. See also Sota, *Partia Komuniste*, pp. 61–62.

[20] Amery, *Sons of the Eagle,* pp. 23–51; Sota, *Partia Komuniste*, p. 62; *Dokumenta Kryesore* I, pp. 478–79, n. 65.

ment, the BK, and the Legality organization. This situation played neatly into the hands of the Germans, who concentrated their troops in the cities and along the strategic roadways and let the contending Albanian factions fight it out in the countryside. The NLM fought a two-front war during the winter of 1943–44. It continued its campaign against the Germans and at the same time undertook actions against the gendarmerie of the Tiranë government, the BK, and the Legality forces.[21] It also stepped up its propaganda offensive against the non-communist groups, which it branded as "traitors" and "collaborationists." The non-communists were also excoriated for concentrating their military efforts against the NLM rather than the Germans.[22]

During the winter of 1943–44, the British Military Mission in Albania labored feverishly to bring the non-communist Albanian groups into the struggle against the Germans and to establish a united front of all the Albanian political groups. This attempt was unsuccessful, since the non-communists were determined to conserve their strength to battle the communists after the liberation. The communists, for their part, were also unwilling to participate in such a venture, which they feared would weaken their chances of seizing power after the war.[23]

[21] For accounts of the NLM military operations during the winter of 1943–44 see Peçi, *Kujtime dhe Dokumente,* I, pp. 93–150; II, pp. 103–28.

[22] For a sampling of pro-communist pamphlets issued between autumn, 1943, and autumn, 1944, see *Thirrje dhe trakte të Partisë Komuniste të Shqipërisë, 1941–1944* ("Appeals and Tracts of the Albanian Communist Party, 1941–1944") (Tiranë: Instituti i Historisë së Partisë Pranë K.Q. të P.P. Sh., 1962), pp. 285–601, docs. 85–189.

[23] Amery, *Sons of the Eagle,* pp. 73 ff; *Dokumenta Kryesore* I, pp. 201–2, doc. 28.

In fact, the communists were so alarmed at the activities of the British that on May 24, 1944, as soon as they had consolidated their position in southern Albania, they convoked a congress at Përmet to insure that control of the NLM would not slip from their grasp. The Congress elected an Anti-Fascist Council of National Liberation to serve as the "supreme executive and legislative organ" for Albania and empowered it to elect an executive committee. Enver Hoxha was chosen chairman of this committee and also appointed Supreme Commander of the Army of National Liberation. This move assured that both military and political power would be concentrated in the hands of the communists if and when the NLM (now renamed the National Liberation Front—NLF) took control of Albania. The Congress also voted to forbid King Zog, whose exile government had never been recognized by the Allies, to return to Albania.[24] In the summer of 1944, crack German troops of the First Mountain Division failed to stop the advancing Albanian Army of National Liberation which, by the end of July, had pressed into central and northern Albania. There the NLF forces met with only token resistance from the demoralized and weakened BK and Legality groups, which had been urged by the British Military Mission not to oppose the NLF advance.[25]

[24] For the activities of the Congress of Përmet ("The First Anti-Fascist Congress of National Liberation") see Sota, *Partia Komuniste*, pp. 68–70 and *Dokumenta Kryesore* I, pp. 211–15, doc. 31. In the proclamation which they issued at the conclusion of the Congress of Përmet, the communists took great pains to assure the Albanian people that while the communists had shown the people the road to liberation, the NLF was not dominated by the communists or any other groups as had been "alleged" by some of "the enemies of the people." See *Gazeta Zyrtare* ("The Official Gazette"), December 21, 1944.

[25] For the final phase of the fighting in Albania during World

With victory in sight, the communists began to increase their ideological and organizational work among the members of the National Liberation Army. The morale and prestige of the Albanian communists also received a boost when the first Soviet military mission arrived in the country in August.[26]

In October, 1944, after about three-fourths of Albania had been liberated, the leaders of the NFL decided to reconvene the Anti-Fascist Congress of National Liberation. The second session of this body met in Berat on October 20, 1944, to plan the last phase of the campaign to free Albania, and to insure that the communists would exercise political power in liberated Albania by transforming the Anti-Fascist National Liberation Committee into the Provisional Democratic Government of Albania. Enver Hoxha was named Prime Minister of this regime.[27]

Within a month after the conclusion of the Congress, Tiranë had fallen to the NLF forces, and by November 29, 1944, the last German troops had been driven from Albanian soil. By this time almost all organized resistance to the communists had been crushed. By virtue of their control of the Provisional Democratic Government, the Army of National Liberation, the NLF, and the National Liberation Councils, the communists were now the undisputed rulers of Albania. Albania, along with Yugoslavia, was one of

---

War II see Peçi, *Kujtime dhe Dokumenta* I, pp. 175–230; II, pp. 138–69; and Amery, *Sons of the Eagle*, pp. 206–301.

[26] Sallabanda, *Kronikë e Ditëve*, pp. 260–61.

[27] Sota, *Partia Komuniste*, pp. 72–77; Dhimo M. Dhima, *Kushtetuta e Republikës Popullore të Shqipërisë* ("The Constitution of the People's Republic of Albania") (Tiranë: Ministria së Arësimit dhe Kulturës, 1960), pp. 49–50. Only two members of the Provisional Democratic Government of Albania were non-communists.

the two party states in Eastern Europe where the communists seized power by their own efforts and her rulers were never to forget this fact.

Albania and the Communist Camp, 1945–48:
The Yugoslav Phase

Albania and Yugoslavia were also the only states in Eastern Europe to fall completely under communist domination prior to the cessation of hostilities in Europe. The primary task confronting the Albanian communists after the expulsion of the German forces in late 1944 was to consolidate their grip on the country. A letter that the Central Committte sent to all Party and military units concluded: "Our main problem now is to remain in power. . . . our immediate [and] principal objective is to establish a new order and to preserve it so that we may go from victory to victory, from reform to reform."[28]

The Albanian communists acted quickly to break the power of the middle class and other potential opponents, to obtain control of the economy, and to eliminate all non-communist foreign influence from Albania. They were in a strong position to execute this program through their control of the government and the military establishment. They had also taken pains to insure that the police and the courts were in the hands of communists, or non-communists "who maintained correct political attitudes."[29]

[28] Foto Çami, *Partia Komuniste e Shqipërisë në luftë për rimëkëmbjen e vendit dhe për zhvillimin e mëtejshëm të revolucionit, 1945–1948* ("The Albanian Communist Party in the Struggle for the Rehabilitation of the Nation and for the Orderly Development of the Revolution, 1945–1948") (Tiranë: Instituti i Historisë së Partisë Pranë K.Q.P.P. Sh., 1958), pp. 14–15.

[29] *Ibid.*, pp. 15–17.

One of the first steps the communists took after the liberation was to try before special tribunals those individuals who were classified as "war criminals." Initially, this designation was applied to the relatively small number of Albanians who had freely collaborated with the Axis and to those who had actively opposed the communists. The terms "war criminal" and "enemy of the people" were later extended to include all who had shown themselves to be openly unsympathetic to the policies of the Provisional Government.[30]

On January 26, 1945, the Council of Ministers created a Special People's Court in Tiranë to try the "major war criminals."[31] This tribunal, under the personal direction of Koçi Xoxe, the Minister of the Interior and next to Hoxha the most powerful figure in the Albanian Communist Party, staged a series of show trials during the early months of 1945 that resulted in hundreds of convictions. Its victims included former government ministers and legislators as well as distinguished patriots whose only crime seemed to have been their refusal to follow without question the dictates of the communist regime. Early in 1945, the communists succeeded in eliminating and discrediting a substantial portion of the pre-war political elite.

The Provisional Government took steps to strengthen its grip on the Albanian economy. In December, 1944, it promulgated a series of laws which provided for strict state regulation of all industrial and commercial enterprises and foreign and domestic trade. These statutes also legalized the confiscation of the real and movable assets of political exiles. A month later, in

[30] Gsovski and Gryzbowski, *Government, Law and Courts*, pp. 172–73.

[31] F. Çami, *Partia Komuniste*, p. 17.

order further to weaken the position of the Albanian middle class, the government enacted an ordinance empowering the state to seize the property of anyone declared "an enemy of the people."[32]

Another measure that did much to cripple the Albanian bourgeoisie was the imposition of a war profits tax in mid-January of 1945. The purpose of this levy, according to the government, was to provide the state with the necessary revenue to undertake reconstruction and improvement projects. In reality it was designed to strike another blow against private enterprise. It succeeded in both objectives. This impost not only accounted for about 50 per cent of the state income in 1945 and 1946, but also resulted in the confiscation of the property of those individuals who found it impossible to pay the assessments levied against them.[33]

During the early part of 1945 the government took its first step toward the nationalization of industry. It confiscated all German and Italian assets in Albania, revoked all foreign economic concessions in the country, nationalized all means of transportation, and created a network of government-sponsored consumer co-operatives.[34]

A more cautious line was adopted toward the peasantry and the agricultural sector of the economy. As the communists realized that they could not remain in

[32] N. Plasari, H. Mara, and V. Misja, *Partia e Punës e Shqipërisë, organizatore e gjithë fitoreve historike të popullit shqiptar* ("The Albanian Party of Labor, Organizer of All of the Historic Victories of the Albanian People") (Tiranë: N. Sh. Botimeve "Naim Frashëri," 1962), p. 62; Skendi, *Albania*, pp. 190, 206, 209.

[33] F. Çami, *Partia Komuniste*, pp. 26–27; Skendi, *Albania*, pp. 190–91.

[34] Plasari, Mara, Misja, *Partia e Punës*, pp. 67–68; F. Çami, *Partia Komuniste*, pp. 25–28.

power without the support of the peasants, they posed as agrarian reformers, inciting the farmers against the landowners. The government canceled all outstanding agricultural debts in January, 1945, and ordered land rental fees reduced by as much as 75 per cent. Water resources were nationalized, making it possible for the farmers to purchase water for their crops from the state at nominal fees.[35] Finally, in August, 1945, the government made public its land reform program, the terms of which were relatively mild. They reflected the desire of the government to gain the confidence of the peasantry, to inspire the farmers to increase their output, and to convince the non-communist nations who were assisting the Albanians through U.N.R.R.A. of the reasonableness of the new Albanian regime.

The Agrarian Reform Law of 1945 nationalized all forests and pasture lands. Land belonging to individuals who had other sources of income was expropriated without compensation. Landowners whose only source of income was derived from farming and who worked their land with modern machinery were allowed to keep up to forty hectares. Religious institutions and landowners solely dependent on agriculture for their livelihood were permitted to retain holdings of twenty hectares. Landless peasants and those who owned less than five hectares received up to five hectares per family unit plus an additional allotment for married sons who were part of the household. The new landowners were required to make nominal compensation to former landowners who were eligible for such payments.[36] Thus, by the end of 1945 the influ-

[35] *Ibid.*, p. 23; Skendi, *Albania*, p. 158.
[36] *Ibid.*, pp. 158–59. The land reform law of 1945 resulted in the redistribution of 155,159 hectares of land, 238,727 olive trees, and 5,923 draft animals to 70,211 "landpoor" and "land-

ence of another segment of the pre-war Albanian political and economic elite, the landowners, was destroyed, while the opposition of the peasantry to the new regime, especially in central and southern Albania, was neutralized at least temporarily.

The Albanian Provisional Government was also striving to gain acceptance both at home and abroad. The triumph of communism in Albania had resulted in the transference of political power from the Gegs to the Tosks. Most of the leading figures in the Albanian communist movement had been Tosks, and since most of the fighting in Albania during World War II had taken place in the southern and south central region of the country, it naturally followed that most of the recruits of the Albanian Army of National Liberation and the Communist Party were drawn from among the Tosks. There were, in fact, only a handful of organized local units of the Albanian Communist Party in north central and northern Albania in 1945.[37] One of the major problems which confronted the regime, therefore, was to extend its authority to northern Albania and to win the confidence of the Gegs, who had a long tradition of opposition to a strong central government. In the period immediately after World War II, a large majority of the Gegs apparently feared and distrusted the new Albanian rulers, who were unknown to them and who espoused doctrines totally alien to their culture.

---

less rural families." *The Development of Agriculture in the People's Republic of Albania* (Tiranë: The State Publishing House "Naim Frashëri," 1962), pp. 8–9.

[37] Bisha, "Nga historia," p. 93. By the end of 1944 the membership of the Albanian Communist Party numbered 5,267. *Ibid.*, p. 88. Perhaps two thirds to three quarters of the Albanian communists were Tosks.

Relations between the Gegs and the Provisional Government were further complicated by the Kosovo question. Nearly all of the Gegs, along with many Albanian nationalists, hoped that the new regime would fight to maintain the 1941 frontiers of the ethnic Albanian state which included the Kosmet. The communists, however, following the repudiation of the Mukaj Pact in 1943, had agreed to restore the Kosmet to Yugoslavia after the war. This understanding was reaffirmed and formalized in January, 1945, with the conclusion of a treaty between the Albanian and Yugoslav governments, which provided that the Kosmet was to be reincorporated into the Yugoslav Federal Republic as an autonomous region.[38] The cession of the Kosmet, coupled with the Provisional Government's domestic policies, served to alienate the Gegs from the new regime in Tiranë. The communists were forced to launch a two-pronged campaign of propaganda and terror in northern Albania to maintain the new order.

The only tangible benefit which accrued to the Provisional Government from its stand on the Kosovo question was that it was recognized by Yugoslavia on April 28, 1945.[39] Yugoslavia was the first nation to take this step, and the Albanians let it be known they hoped that other states, both communist and non-communist, would follow suit. The expressed desire of the dominant faction of the Albanian Communist Party to seek

[38] Charlotte Saikowski, "Albania in Soviet Satellite Policy, 1945–1953" (unpublished thesis for the Certificate of the Russian Institute, Columbia University, 1954), p. 13.

[39] *White Book on the Aggressive Activities by the Governments of the U.S.S.R., Poland, Czechoslovakia, Hungary, Rumania and Albania Towards Yugoslavia* (Beograd: Ministry of Foreign Affairs of the Federal People's Republic of Yugoslavia, 1951), doc. 59, pp. 164–65 (hereafter cited as *Yugoslav White Book*).

ties with the West as well as the East had caused much consternation in Belgrade. Tito and his colleagues now realized that they would have to step up their activities in Albania to assure that Albania remain securely within their grasp. Nevertheless, the Albanian government proceeded to explore with the United States and Great Britain the possibility of establishing diplomatic relations. Both Washington and London responded favorably to this overture. By the late spring of 1945 their representatives were already in Albania.[40]

In order to legitimatize the position of the Provisional Government and to convince the Western Powers of their intention to establish a democratic regime in Albania, the communists began to make preparations for the convocation of a Constituent Assembly. In early August, 1945, the National Liberation Front held a Congress in Tiranë to map out the strategy of the pro-government supporters during the electoral campaign. At this meeting the NLF was rechristened the Democratic Front (DF). This new organization was, as in the other states of Eastern Europe, nothing more than a front for the communist party, which as yet was not confident enough of its position to make a direct appeal to the people. The DF, however, was completely dominated by the communist party. At its August Congress, the DF drew up a list of candidates, comprised largely of communists and communist sympathizers, to run in the election, which had been scheduled for December.[41]

During the election campaign, the Albanian au-

---

[40] Stephen D. Kertesz, ed., *The Fate of East Central Europe: Hopes and Failures of American Foreign Policy* (Notre Dame, Indiana: University of Notre Dame Press, 1956), p. 305.

[41] *Dokumenta Kryesore* I, pp. 246–49, doc. 39; Skendi, *Albania*, p. 87.

thorities went to great lengths to convince the Western Powers that there was freedom of thought and expression in Albania by permitting them to distribute literature and show films and by allowing their representatives to circulate freely about the country. The Provisional Government noted with pride that Albanian authors and poets of all shades of political opinion had been invited to participate in organizing a Writers' Union in October 1945,[42] but chose to overlook the fact that despite the protests of many of the non-communist members of the DF, a law promulgated on October 1, 1945 made it extremely difficult for any candidate to run in opposition to the DF slate.[43]

In early November at the Fourth Plenum of the Central Committee, the Albanian Communist Party formally agreed to mobilize its resources to secure the election of the candidates of the Front. To ensure the victory of the DF slate, the communists used a variety of methods ranging from propaganda to outright terror.[44] The prestige of the Front, which campaigned in support of the policies of the Provisional Government, was enhanced when the latter was recognized by the Soviet Union on November 10, 1945.

In the election of December 2, 1945, 89.8 per cent of the eligible voters went to the polls and 93.2 percent of these cast their ballots for the slate of the DF.[45] The Constituent Assembly began its deliberations on January 10, 1945. A day later it formally abolished the

[42] Skendi, *Albania*, pp. 23, 312–13. Interview with Mr. Harry Fultz, November 8, 1959.

[43] Gsovski and Grzybowski, *Government, Law and Courts*, p. 174; F. Çami, *Partia Komuniste*, p. 32.

[44] *Dokumenta Kryesore* I, pp. 263–68, doc. 44; Gsovski and Grzybowski, *Government, Law and Courts*, pp. 174–75.

[45] *Anuari Statistikor, 1961*, p. 48.

monarchy and proclaimed Albania a People's Republic. After several months of acrimonious debate between the DF moderates and conservatives, a new
Albanian Constitution was drawn up. This document
was a virtual carbon of the Yugoslav Constitution of
1945, with the major exception that the federal structure of Yugoslavia was not adopted.[46]

The dispute between the moderate and hard-line
factions of the DF reflected the cleavage which was developing within the ranks of the Party itself and which
had been a topic of discussion at the meeting of the
Fourth Plenum of the Central Committee the previous
November. On this occasion the Party leadership had
noted that the position of the Albanian communist
movement was imperiled by two major factors: the
assistance and encouragement which the anti-communist elements in Albanian were receiving from "foreign
reactionary powers" and the fact that the Party and
the DF "were riddled with opportunists." Both of these
problems would have to be overcome, it was decided,
if the communists were to maintain their dominant
position in Albania. In order to purify the ranks of the
Party, the Central Committee ordered all communists
to turn in their party cards until their status could be
clarified. The review of the Party membership, which
took place between November 1945 and June 1946,
resulted in the expulsion of 1246 individuals, roughly
10 per cent of those then on the Party rolls.[47]

[46] For a discussion of the main features of the Constitution of
1946 see F. Çami, *Partia Komuniste*, pp. 37–39 and Skendi, *Albania*, pp. 62–65. Following the adoption of the Constitution,
the Constituent Assembly transformed itself into a parliamentary
body (the People's Assembly) and continued to sit until the 1950
elections.

[47] *Dokumenta Kryesore* I, pp. 264–67, doc. 44; p. 482, n. 86;
F. Çami, *Partia Komuniste*, pp. 32–34.

The major source of friction within the Party stemmed from the fact that Sejfulla Malëshova and the moderates were urging the government to pursue an independent course in foreign affairs under which Albania would maintain friendly relations with both the communist and the western camps. They also advocated the creation of a broad, truly national political front in which all spectra of political opinion would be represented and the postponement of socialization in Albania until the agricultural and industrial sectors of the economy had been further developed within a capitalist framework. These policies, which could very well have resulted in the weakening of the communists' hold on Albania and undermined Yugoslav influence in the country, were unacceptable to the militant factions of both the Albanian and the Yugoslav Parties.[48]

Hoxha, who up until this time seems to have been sympathetic to the views of the moderates, began to waver under pressure from the Yugoslavs and their spokesman in the Albanian Party, Xoxe. Realizing the weakness of his own position, he joined forces with the pro-Yugoslav clique at a meeting of the Politburo which was held between December 6 and 11, and denounced the stand of Malëshova and the moderates.[49]

The stage was now set for the showdown between the militants and the moderates which took place on February 21, 1946, at the Sixth Plenum of the Central Committee. There was little doubt as to what the out-

[48] *Dokumenta Kryesore* I, pp. 334–40, doc. 50; Plasari, Mara, Misja, *Partia e Punës*, pp. 94–95; F. Çami, *Partia Komuniste,* pp. 55–59. The Albanian moderates were comprised mainly of intellectuals and civil servants while the militants were drawn largely from the working-class elements of the Party.

[49] Dedijer, *Marredhanjet jugosllavo-shqiptare*, pp. 145–46, 150–51; *Dokumenta Kryesore* I, p. 269.

come of this meeting would be, since Xoxe, acting in his dual capacity as Minister of the Interior and Party Organizational Secretary, had already initiated a purge of those individuals suspected of pro-Malëshova or anti-Yugoslav tendencies in accordance with the decrees of the November, 1945, plenum of Central Committee. The Sixth Plenum "unanimously" condemned the views of Malëshova and expelled him from the Politburo and the Central Committee. The Central Committee also decreed that Albanian foreign policy should be oriented toward that of the Soviet Union and the People's Democracies, that the tempo of the nationalization of industry should increase, that more radical agricultural reforms should be undertaken, that the voluntary establishment of collective farms should be encouraged, that the private sector of the economy should be more strictly controlled, that ideological work in both the Party and the DF should be intensified, and that a program of social reform should be undertaken immediately. The Sixth Plenum also recommended that the Party convene its First Congress on May 25, 1946.[50]

Thus by the spring of 1946, with the adoption of the new Constitution and with the destruction of the moderate wing of the Party, the communists had consolidated their position in Albania. In accordance with the terms of the 1946 Constitution, the People's Assembly elected a new cabinet. The most powerful individual in this government, at least on paper, was Enver Hoxha, who occupied the posts of Prime Minister, Foreign Minister, Defense Minister, and Commander-in-Chief of the Armed Forces. He also continued to

[50] *Ibid.*, p. 482, n. 86; pp. 270–78, doc. 45.

serve as Secretary General of the Communist Party. His principal rival, Koçi Xoxe, retained the Ministry of the Interior as well as his position as Party Organizational Secretary.

Sensing the threat that Xoxe and the Yugoslavs posed to him, Hoxha immediately sought to free himself from their clutches. His efforts, however, ended in failure. Xoxe and the Yugoslavs thwarted his plans to call the Party Congress scheduled for May, perhaps because they feared that this body might take an anti-Yugoslav stand.[51] The Soviet government sidetracked his request to visit Moscow,[52] and the Albanian Politburo rebuffed his draft of a resolution condemning the policies of Yugoslavia in Albania during and after World War II.[53] At the same time, Albania's relations with the Western Powers were beginning to deteriorate as a result of the renewed Greek demand for incorporation of southern Albanian provinces (Northern Epirus) into Greece, and because the West lacked enthusiasm for the new Albanian regime.

Confronted with opposition at home and hostility and indifference from abroad, Hoxha finally capitulated to Yugoslav pressures for the establishment of closer ties between Tiranë and Belgrade. In July, 1946, he led a high-level Albanian delegation to the Yugoslav capital, where on July 9, a Treaty of Friendship, Cooperation and Mutual Aid was concluded between the two states. This treaty was followed by a series of technical and economic pacts, the most important of

[51] *Ibid.*, p. 269.
[52] Vladimir Dedijer, *Tito* (New York: Simon and Schuster, 1953), p. 273.
[53] *Dokumenta Kryesore* I, pp. 382–83, doc. 56; F. Çami, *Partia Komuniste*, pp. 105–107.

which were the Joint Company and the Economic Cooperation Agreements of November 28, 1946.[54] While Tiranë did receive some much-needed diplomatic and economic support as a result of these treaties, they nevertheless had the effect of transforming Albania, with the apparent approval of the Soviet Union, into a Yugoslav satellite. The difficulties which were to develop between Albania and Yugoslavia on the one hand and Yugoslavia and the Soviet Union on the other had their origins in 1946, when Tito apparently began to feel that the agreements he had concluded with Hoxha gave him the green light to prepare the way for the incorporation of Albania into Yugoslavia.

While Albania was drifting into the Yugoslav orbit during the summer of 1946, its relations with the Western Powers continued to worsen. In the early months of 1946, the Albanian government restricted the movements of the U.S. and British missions in the country on suspicion that they were working in close harmony with the few active anti-communist groups in Albania. Great Britain announced in April, 1946, that she would not send a diplomatic mission to Tiranë and that she would not permit the Albanians to establish a legation in London. Prospects for the establishment of U.S.–Albanian relations were likewise shattered by the passage of the Pepper Resolution in the United States Senate by a unanimous voice vote on July 29, 1946.[55] This act, which placed the Senate on record as favoring the award of Northern Epirus to Greece, presented the communists with a potent tool with which to build up anti-American sentiment in

[54] *Yugoslav White Book*, p. 165, doc. 59; Skendi, *Albania*, pp. 353–54.

[55] U.S., *Congressional Record*, 79th Cong., 2d Sess., 1946, XCII, Part 8, p. 10336.

Albania. It also provided them with a convenient excuse to reject on August 13, 1946, the American stipulation that the recognition of all existing bilateral treaties was a prerequisite for the resumption of diplomatic relations between the two nations. Despite the fact that Secretary of State Byrnes had been instrumental in securing the withdrawal of the Northern Epirus question from the agenda of the Paris Peace Conference, Albania continued and even intensified its anti-American propaganda during the autumn of 1946. Confronted with the growing hostility of the Albanian regime and the rejection of her conditions for recognition, the United States recalled her mission from Albania on November 6, 1946.[56]

In retrospect it now appears that Hoxha was, at least in part, forced into taking a strong anti-Western stand by Xoxe and the Yugoslavs, who feared that the presence of the United States in Albania might have posed a threat to their plans for an Albanian-Yugoslav union. Furthermore, the East-West rift, which had become evident by 1946, probably also made it necessary for Hoxha to take a hard-line stance toward the West. Finally, the Greek demands concerning Northern Epirus, the outbreak of a series of small-scale uprisings in Albania in which the representatives of the United States and Britain were alleged to have been involved, and the refusal of the United States and Great Britain to support the Albanian request for admission into the United Nations may have convinced Hoxha of the dangers of continuing his flirtation with the West.

Albania's steady movement into the Communist Bloc was also reflected in her domestic policies during 1946, when the tempo of socialization was increased.

[56] *New York Times*, November 7, 1946.

By the summer of 1946, virtually all Albanian-owned industries were nationalized, most domestic wholesale and retail trade was state controlled, foreign trade was made a government monopoly, and a currency reform was enacted that further weakened the position of the middle class. The state also began to pursue a tougher line toward the peasantry by prohibiting the sale and transfer of land and by increasing pressure on farmers to form agricultural collectives. Thus, by the end of 1946, the foundations for a socialist society had been laid in Albania.[57]

The Albanian economy, however, still remained precarious. That Albania had managed to survive during 1945 and 1946 was in large measure due to the generous assistance amounting to $26,250,900 she had received from U.N.R.R.A.[58] Hoxha, who realized that the economy of his country was incapable of meeting the needs of his people, let alone finance the modernization of agriculture and the expansion of industry, was forced to turn to Yugoslavia for help. Like Mussolini in the 1920s and 1930s, Tito sought to take advantage of Albania's economic weakness and to transform the country into a Yugoslav colony.

The Yugoslavs began to play an increasingly important role in Albanian affairs after the conclusion of the Treaty of Friendship, Cooperation and Mutual Aid with Albania on July 9, 1946. This pact provided for the establishment of an agency to coordinate the

[57] For details, see Vladimir Misja, *Krijimi dhe zhvillimi i industrë në R. P. Sh.* (Tiranë: N. Sh. Botimere "Naim Frashëri," 1963), pp. 91–92; Plasari, Mara, Misja, *Partia e Punës,* pp. 70–74; F. Çami, *Partia Komuniste,* pp. 61–66.

[58] For an analysis of U.N.R.R.A. aid to Albania see George Woodbridge, *U.N.R.R.A., The History of the United Nations Relief and Rehabilitation Administration,* 3 vols. (New York: Columbia University Press, 1950), III, pp. 428, 430–33.

economic plans of the signatories, for the standardization of the Albanian and Yugoslav monetary systems, and for the creation of a common price system and customs union between the two nations. The two economic systems were merged for all practical purposes.

When it came to implementation of these agreements, however, misunderstandings between Albania and Yugoslavia arose from their conflicting interests. The Albanians hoped that the assistance from the Yugoslavs would enable them to become economically independent, while Tito, on the other hand, hoped to strengthen his grip on Albania by making it dependent upon Yugoslavia.

During the early part of 1947, the Albanian government raised objections over such matters as the value which the Yugoslavs had assigned to Albanian raw material exports to Yugoslavia, the method by which the Albanian investment in the joint companies would be calculated, the alleged failure of the Yugoslavs to supply their full share of the capital for the joint companies, and the fact that the Albanian-Yugoslav shipping company sought to assume control of Albania's foreign trade. In addition, the Albanians also complained bitterly about the activities of the Yugoslav advisers and technicians, whom they charged with attempting to sabotage the Albanian economy, in order to discredit the leaders of the Party and Government and thus pave the way for their replacement with individuals who would be more willing to take orders from Belgrade.[59]

[59] *Lufta e Partisë së Punës së Shqipërisë kundër ndërhyrjes armiqësore të udhëheqjes revizioniste të L.K.J. në punët e brendëshme të vendit tonë* ("The Struggle of the Albanian Party of Labor Against the Unfriendly Intervention of the Revisionist Leadership of the Y.L.C. Into the Internal Affairs of Our Coun-

By April, 1947, relations between the two nations had become so strained that the Albanians felt it necessary to dispatch to Belgrade a special mission headed by Nako Spiru, Chairman of the State Planning Commission. The Albanian delegation was instructed to obtain from the Yugoslavs a pledge of assistance in creating light consumer industries and a petroleum refinery, as well as to negotiate a trade agreement for 1947. Albania had initiated a Nine-Month Economic Plan for 1947 and the prospects of fulfilling the industrial goals of the Plan were bleak without Yugoslav aid. The Yugoslavs, who fully appreciated the predicament of the Albanians, refused to discuss the Spiru proposals until the Albanians would agree to the formation of a joint commission to coordinate the economic plans of the two nations, as had been stipulated in the treaty of July, 1946. Hoxha refused the Yugoslav request.[60]

At this point the Yugoslavs, weary of Albanian complaints, proposed that the two nations draw up a joint Five-Year Plan to be administered by a bilateral commission headquartered in Tiranë. Belgrade agreed to supply Tiranë with twenty billion dinars ($400 million) in aid to develop Albanian agricultural and mineral resources. Spiru and his colleagues remained cool toward this scheme, pointing out that this plan doomed Albania to remain a backward nation, bound forever to Yugoslavia.

Spiru's suspicions regarding the true intentions of Belgrade toward his homeland were aroused when the

---

try") (Tiranë: Drejtorisë së Propagandës e Agitasionit të K.Q. të P.P. Sh., 1958), pp. 17–21 (hereafter cited as *Lufta P.P. Sh. kundër LKJ*).

[60] For a summary of the Spiru mission see *ibid.*, pp. 22–27.

Yugoslav government proposed that the two states sign a secret pact which would protect the interests of Yugoslavia in Albania in the event that there should be a change of government in Tiranë. This overture was rejected by Spiru, and it served to reinforce his conviction that Yugoslavia was far more interested in obtaining a favored position in Albania than in strengthening the communist regime there. Thus, instead of improving Yugoslav-Albanian relations, the Spiru mission had succeeded only in exacerbating them.

Shortly after the return of Spiru, the Albanian government formally rejected the Yugoslav proposal to draw up a joint Five-Year Plan.[61] The Yugoslavs, acting through Xoxe, then launched a new offensive against those elements in the Albanian Communist Party whom they considered hostile to their policies. On May 20, 1947, the Albanian government announced that nine members of the People's Assembly who had been known for their opposition to the Yugoslavs had been arrested, tried, and convicted of plotting against the state.[62] Boshnjaku and Malëshova were among them. This action, undoubtedly initiated by Xoxe, was probably designed to intimidate Hoxha, Spiru, and others in the Albanian Party who had displayed a reluctance to accept the Yugoslav program for Albania.

In the early part of June, 1947, the pressure on the leadership of the Albanian Party was intensified when the Central Committee of the Yugoslav Communist Party accused Hoxha of pursuing an independent

---

[61] F. Çami, *Partia Komuniste*, p. 112.

[62] Martin Ebon, *World Communism Today* (New York: Whittlesey House, Inc., 1948), pp. 155–56; Hugh Seton-Watson, *The East European Revolution* (New York: Frederick A. Praeger, 1956), p. 227.

course in foreign and domestic policies and of fostering anti-Yugoslav sentiments among the Albanian people. This gambit succeeded only in triggering off a new wave of hostility toward Belgrade. Over the opposition of Xoxe and his chief collaborator, Pandi Kristo, the statement of the Yugoslav Central Committee was denounced by the Albanian Politburo as another attempt by Belgrade to interfere in the internal affairs of the Albanian Party.[63]

The Yugoslav government, which at this time appears to have had some second thoughts concerning the wisdom of its hard-line policy toward Albania, now reversed its tactics. On July 12, 1947, the Yugoslavs agreed to make available to Albania a credit of two billion dinars ($40 million) for the year 1947. The Yugoslav grant, which represented 58 per cent of the Albanian state income for that year,[64] would provide Tito with an effective weapon with which to keep the recalcitrant Albanians in line.

At this point, Hoxha, now beginning to appreciate the weakness of his own position, once again turned to the Soviet Union for assistance to lessen the dependency of his government on Yugoslavia.

The Soviet Union, which was certainly privy to the situation in Albania, does not appear to have consulted with Belgrade prior to extending an invitation to Hoxha to visit Moscow.[65] The Soviet Union pledged to construct several factories (textile and sugar mills, etc.) in Albania and to provide the Albanians with agricultural and industrial machinery.[66]

[63] F. Çami, *Partia Komuniste,* p. 111–12; *Lufta P.P. Sh. kundër LKJ*, pp. 38–39.

[64] Dedijer, *Tito*, p. 302.

[65] *Lufta P.P. Sh. kundër LKJ*, p. 31–32.

[66] *Ibid.*, pp. 38–39; F. Çami, *Partia Komuniste*, pp. 111–13.

The reception of the Albanian delegation in Moscow and the grant of a credit to Albania, coupled with the unwillingness of the Soviet government to make the Yugoslavs a party to their discussions with the Albanians or even to inform Belgrade of what had transpired, seems to have constituted a warning to Tito that Moscow was not wholly in accord with his policies in Albania. The promise of Soviet aid for the development of light industry in Albania had the effect of refuting the Yugoslav contention that such a step was both unnecessary and impractical. Stalin was not yet ready in mid-1947 to rebuke the Yugoslavs openly for their conduct in Albania, nor was he prepared to dislodge them from their favored position there. He apparently wished only to make clear the fact that he was the master of the communist camp and that he would make the final decision concerning the precise role of Yugoslavia in Albania.

Stalin, in the summer of 1947, was probably also reluctant to unduly antagonize Yugoslavia because it might have jeopardized the creation of the Cominform. Tito had been delegated a large degree of responsibility for laying the organizational groundwork for this body. The Soviet dictator may have believed that the Cominform would provide him with a potent weapon with which to control the Yugoslavs in the future, should they step out of line in Albania or elsewhere.

It is interesting to note that Albania was not invited to participate in the organizational meeting of the Cominform in September, 1947, nor was she later admitted to membership in it.[67] There are probably several factors that account for this. First of all, Tito may have insisted that Albania be excluded on the grounds

[67] Adam B. Ulam, *Titoism and the Cominform* (Cambridge: Harvard University Press, 1952), p. 49.

that the Yugoslavs, who enjoyed a favored position in Albania, were capable of representing the interests of the Albanians. Secondly, the Soviet Union, which may have harbored doubts concerning the loyalty of the Albanian Communist Party to Moscow, might have suggested that Albania be excluded from the Cominform. If, as has been implied, the Cominform was conceived at least in part as a device by which Moscow could control the activities of Tito, the Albanian Party, which was subject to Yugoslav influence, could hardly be an effective member of the organization. Finally, there was also the danger that if the pro-Tito faction ever gained control of the Albanian Party and government, a pro-Yugoslav clique might emerge in the Cominform. In any event, the exclusion of Albania from the Cominform does serve to indicate the unique and insignificant position of Albania in the communist camp in 1947.

Albanian-Yugoslav relations continued to deteriorate during the autumn of 1947. In defiance of the wishes of Belgrade, the Albanian government prepared an economic plan stressing the development of light industry and the modernization of agriculture and concluded a trade agreement with Bulgaria in August, 1947.[68] The Yugoslavs, who now feared that their position in Albania was seriously threatened, dispatched a strong letter to the Central Committee of the Albanian Communist Party in November, 1947. On this occasion, Marshall Tito singled out Nako Spiru for criticism. He blamed Spiru for the "misunderstandings" which had arisen between Albania and Yugoslavia and branded him a "traitor." Spiru now became the prime target of the Xoxe clique, and when none of the hier-

[68] *Lufta P.P. Sh. kundër LKJ*, p. 27; Skendi, *Albania*, p. 352.

archy of the Albanian Party publicly came to his defense, Spiru committed suicide in the latter part of November, 1947.[69]

If Tito had hoped to cow the Albanians into submission by his note of November, 1947, he was disappointed. In December, 1947, Hoxha, probably after consulting with the Soviet government, went to Sofia where he concluded a Treaty of Friendship, Cooperation and Mutual Assistance with the Bulgarian government. This was the second such agreement which the Albanians had signed, the first being with Yugoslavia in June, 1946. This pact, insofar as the Albanians were concerned, may have been signed to refute Tito's contention that Yugoslavia enjoyed a privileged position in Albania. In order to correct this impression, the Yugoslavs through Xoxe sought to have inserted in the treaty a clause which in effect stated that any joint action undertaken by Albania and Bulgaria should have prior Yugoslav approval. Although Xoxe in a midnight confrontation with Hoxha threatened to disrupt the ceremony at which the pact would be signed, Hoxha remained firm and forced his pro-Yugoslav colleague to back down. During his stay in Sofia Hoxha also enraged the Yugoslavs by his failure to mention the name of Tito in public.[70]

By the beginning of 1948, the deepening Albanian-Yugoslav crisis had become an important factor in the growing rift between the Soviet Union and Yugoslavia. In January of that year Milovan Djilas journeyed to Moscow at Stalin's request to discuss the Albanian problem. The Soviet government, which had already expressed its displeasure to Belgrade over the forma-

[69] *Dokumenta Kryesore* I, pp. 443–45, doc. 50; F. Çami, *Partia Komuniste*, pp. 114–16.

[70] *Lufta P.P. Sh. kundër LKJ*, pp. 32–33.

tion of the joint Albanian-Yugoslav companies and the presence of the large group of Yugoslav military and economic advisors in Albanian, was now probably seeking to entice Tito into making a move of a compromising nature in Albania. Upon arriving in Moscow, Djilas was informed by Stalin and Molotov, who were obviously toying with him, that the Soviet Union had no objection to Yugoslavia's "swallowing" Albania and that Moscow agreed with Belgrade that the "proletarian" Xoxe was far more preferable than the "Westernized intellectual" Hoxha.[71]

Stalin did not have to wait long for the trap to spring. In early February, after having scuttled the Tito-Dimitrov plan for a Balkan Federation, the Soviet dictator learned that the Yugoslavs had moved an air squadron into Albania and that they were planning to dispatch two divisions there in order to bolster up the defenses of Albania against a threatened Greek invasion. Stalin, who realized that the projected Yugoslav action represented nothing more than a preliminary step toward the absorption of Albania into Yugoslavia, castigated the Yugoslavs for having the audacity to take this action without first consulting him. Molotov then joined the affray by threatening to issue a public statement condemning this move unless the Yugoslavs agreed to abandon this project. Stalin also insisted later that month that Belgrade shelve its plans to incorporate Albania until after a Bulgarian-Yugoslav federation had been effected. Finally, Stalin, who by now had become quite apprehensive over Tito's ambitions in the Balkans, urged that the Greek Civil War be terminated, since the communists had no hope of toppling

[71] Milovan Djilas, *Conversations with Stalin* (New York: Harcourt, Brace and World, 1962), pp. 133–47; Dedijer, *Tito*, pp. 304, 309–11.

the Monarchy. The continuation of hostilities, he argued, might result in Western intervention in the Balkans.[72]

In Albania, meanwhile, the worsening Soviet-Yugoslav crisis was reflected by the unleashing of a new offensive by Xoxe and the Yugoslavs in defiance of the dictates of Stalin. Xoxe had inaugurated the campaign in December, 1947, with a speech he delivered at the Party training school in Tiranë, in which he catalogued the errors of the Albanian government and Party in their relations with Yugoslavia. The Yugoslav Central Committee, in early 1948, had sent a special emissary, Savo Zllatić, to Albania to work with Xoxe for the convocation of a meeting of the Central Committee to bring about a reorientation of Albanian policy and to prepare the way for Albanian-Yugoslav union.[73]

The Eighth Plenum of the Central Committee of the Albanian Communist Party, which was in session between February 26 and March 8, 1948, marked the high tide of Yugoslav influence in Albania. The decisions of the Eighth Plenum represented a victory for Xoxe and his supporters. Hoxha was forced to admit his past errors, and he joined in the chorus which denounced Spiru for having poisoned Albanian-Yugoslav relations. It was only by performing this act of self-criticism that Hoxha was able to retain his position as Party Secretary General. The Plenum expelled a number of prominent Party members, including Liri Belishova, the widow of Spiru. Mehmet Shehu, the Moscow-trained Chief of the Albanian General Staff

[72] F. Çami, *Partia Komuniste*, pp. 119–20; Djilas, *Conversations*, pp. 171–83.

[73] *Lufta P.P. Sh. kundër LKJ*, pp. 43–44; *Dokumenta Kryesore* I, p. 484, n. 96.

and an opponent of the plan to merge the Albanian and Yugoslav armies, was relieved of his command and dropped as a candidate member of the Central Committee. The Plenum then dutifully approved Xoxe's proposals to merge the Albanian and Yugoslav economies and armed forces.[74]

In the weeks immediately following the conclusion of the Eighth Plenum Xoxe and the Yugoslavs worked feverishly to consolidate their position in Albania. Behind the scenes Xoxe made preparation for a series of purge trials by which he expected to eliminate Hoxha and the other leaders of the anti-Yugoslav faction of the Party. The Yugoslavs sent a commission to Tiranë to coordinate the economies of the two countries. They also demanded that the joint companies be placed under the exclusive control of Belgrade. Tito also demanded that the Soviet military mission in Albania be expelled and that the unification of the Albanian and Yugoslav military services take place immediately.[75]

Xoxe, apparently confident he had gained the upper hand in his struggle with Hoxha, called in April a meeting of the Politburo, where he proposed that Albania petition Belgrade for admission into the Yugoslav Federal Republic. The pro-Hoxha majority in the Politburo refused to approve this scheme. Xoxe then decided to whip up popular sentiment for his plan by resorting to a campaign of propaganda and terror. His efforts, however, had come too late.[76]

Yugoslav prestige in Albania had begun to wane as

[74] For a discussion of the proceedings of the Eighth Plenum of the Central Committee of the Albanian Communist Party see *ibid.*, pp. 388–91, doc. 56; pp. 445–46, doc. 58; F. Çami, *Partia Komuniste*, pp. 116–18; *Lufta P.P. Sh. kundër LKJ*, pp. 43–46.

[75] *Ibid.*, pp. 45–46; F. Çami, *Partia Komuniste*, pp. 118–19.

[76] *Ibid.*, pp. 119–20.

the Soviet-Yugoslav dispute worsened. Hoxha now felt confident enough to attack and insult the Yugoslavs publicly. He absented himself from the reception held in honor of Tito's birthday on May 25, 1948, and following the example of the other East European leaders, save Dimitrov, he did not even send greetings to the Yugoslav dictator on this occasion. Three weeks later he ordered the Yugoslavs to close their information center in Tiranë and banned the sale of *Borba* in Albania.[77]

When news of the Yugoslav expulsion from the Cominform leaked out on June 28, 1948, the Albanian leaders realized that the opportunity to shake themselves free from Tito's grasp had arrived. They may have also felt that by taking a quick and decisive stand against Tito they would convince Stalin of their loyalty. At any rate, Albania was the first of the communist states of Eastern Europe to attack Yugoslavia. On July 1, 1948, the Albanian government denounced all of the economic agreements which it had made with Yugoslavia on the grounds that they were incompatible with Albania's status as a sovereign and independent state. The Treaty of Friendship and Mutual Aid of 1946 was left in force in order "to serve as the basis for the development of correct relations between our two friendly and brotherly peoples in the future."[78] The Albanians then ordered all Yugoslav specialists and advisers to leave the country within 48 hours, placed the Yugoslav legation under continuous surveillance, and forbade the Yugoslavs to distribute any literature or other materials in Albania. The Albanian press and radio now launched a propaganda offensive against

[77] Saikowski, "Albania in Soviet Satellite Policy," p. 25; *New York Times*, July 2, 1948.

[78] *Yugoslav White Book,* pp. 304–5, doc. 188.

Tito, which has continued with but few interruptions until today.[79]

While the Soviet-Yugoslav and the Albanian-Yugoslav splits were responsible for the preservation of Albanian independence and the Hoxha faction of the Party, they did create some serious problems for Hoxha. Albania was not an economically viable state. Would the Soviet Union now take up the Yugoslav burden in Albania? Hoxha, who had shown a certain degree of independence in his relations with Tito, must have also wondered whether Stalin would cast him aside, now that he had served his purpose, in favor of a more pliant leader who would follow the dictates of Moscow. Hoxha's fears were quickly laid to rest. In September, 1948, the Soviet government, which at this point had no desire to do anything that might cause Albania to slip back into Tito's fold, concluded an economic agreement with Albania to compensate for the loss of Yugoslav aid and gave Hoxha a vote of confidence.[80]

The Albanian dictator now felt strong enough to move against the pro-Yugoslav elements in the Albanian Party. At a meeting (the Eleventh Plenum) of the Central Committee in mid-September, 1948, Hoxha renewed his attack on the Yugoslavs and the Xoxe clique. The Eleventh Plenum denounced the decisions of the Eighth Plenum and restored Mehmet Shehu and Liri Belishova, as well as those other party members who had been "unjustly" purged by Xoxe, to their former government and Party positions. Xoxe himself, who had now taken an anti-Yugoslav stance, lost his job as Party Organizational Secretary but was allowed

[79]*Ibid.*, pp. 164–73, doc. 59.
[80] William E. Griffith, *Albania and the Sino-Soviet Rift* (Cambridge: The M.I.T. Press, 1963), p. 21.

to continue as a member of the Politburo. Similarly mild punishment was meted out to Xoxe's leading henchmen. The Plenum instructed the government to strengthen its relations with the Soviet Union. Finally, the Plenum approved the change of the name of the Albanian Communist Party to the Albanian Party of Labor and set November, 1948, as the date for the long-delayed First Congress of the Albanian Party.[81]

Hoxha continued his drive against Xoxe and his clique in the interlude between the Eleventh Plenum and the First Congress of the APL. On October 3, he reshuffled his cabinet by removing Xoxe as Minister of the Interior and transferring him to the Ministry of Industry. The Ministry of the Interior was given to one of Xoxe's confidants, Nesti Kerenexhi, in order to lull the former into a sense of security. Then, on October 31, the ax fell. Xoxe and his lieutenants, including Kerenexhi, were stripped of their government posts. Mehmet Shehu, who had previously been restored to his position as Chief of the Army General Staff, was appointed Minister of the Interior. This latter step was probably taken to gain the support of the army for Hoxha.[82] The Albanian dictator was now preparing to deliver the *coup de grace* to Xoxe and his clique at the First Party Congress.

The First Congress of the APL met in Tiranë from November 8 to November 22, 1948. It was attended by 862 delegates representing 45,382 members and

[81] For the proceedings of the Eleventh Plenum of the Central Committee of the Albanian Communist Party see *Dokumenta Kryesore* I, pp. 376–404, doc. 56.

[82] For a summary of the events between the Eleventh Plenum and the First Congress of the Albanian Party of Labor see Hamm, *Albania—China's Beachhead*, pp. 95–96; "History of the Albanian Communist Party II," *News from Behind the Iron Curtain*, V, No. 1 (January 1956), p. 28.

candidate members. At the Congress, Enver Hoxha was renamed Secretary General of the Party, and a new Central Committee of twenty-one members and ten candidates was chosen. The new Central Committee was naturally comprised of pro-Hoxha stalwarts. In his report to the Congress, Hoxha acknowledged the mistakes that the Party had made in the past and blamed these on the influence of the Yugoslavs and Xoxe. He outlined his plans for the development of industry in Albania, the strengthening of Soviet-Albanian relations, and the improvement of the organization and ideological level of the Party. Hoxha then called for and obtained the expulsion of Xoxe and his closest associate, Pandi Kristo, from the Party.[83]

By the end of 1948, Albania, under the leadership of Enver Hoxha, had taken her place as a member of the Soviet Commonwealth in Eastern Europe. Prior to 1948, Albania had been a satellite of Yugoslavia. She did not have any direct treaty ties with the Soviet Union. She occupied a unique position in the communist camp—that of a sub-satellite. The Stalin-Tito break in 1948 enabled Albania to escape from Yugoslav tutelege and to enter into direct relations with the Soviet Union and the other communist states of Eastern Europe.

It is interesting to note that while both the Yugoslav revolt against the Soviet Union and the Albanian revolt against Yugoslavia were to a large extent fostered by nationalism, the Albanians were not to enjoy the same degree of independence as the Yugoslavs, since Albania had to rely on the U.S.S.R. for economic assistance as well as for diplomatic and even possibly

[83] For the proceedings of the First Congress of the Albanian Party of Labor see *Dokumenta Kryesore* I, p. 405; pp. 423–65, doc. 58.

military support in order to survive as a separate communist state. In 1948, however, the Albanians were far more willing to subordinate themselves to Moscow than to Belgrade. The Soviet Union was geographically remote and did not threaten to absorb Albania physically. In addition, the U.S.S.R. was better able than Yugoslavia to supply Albania with the material and technical assistance required to build a socialist industrial society.

Insofar as Stalin was concerned, he realized that the communist leaders of Albania, surrounded as they were by hostile neighbors and isolated from the West, could not long remain in power without the patronage of the Soviet Union. This fact alone ensured the subservience of Albania to Moscow. But, in 1948, Soviet policy toward Albania was motivated by a more pressing and immediate consideration—the desire to prevent the formation of a pro-Yugoslav faction within the world communist movement.

3: THE INTENSIVE SOCIALIST DEVELOPMENT OF ALBANIA: STALINISM, 1949–53

Following the Soviet-Yugoslav break, Albania began to play a more active, if still limited, role in the affairs of the Communist Bloc. Although Albania had not been invited to participate in the establishment of the Council for Mutual Economic Assistance (COMECON) in January, 1949, she applied for and was granted membership in that organization the following month. This meant that the satellite states of Eastern Europe were required to aid the Soviet Union in the task of developing the Albanian economy. During the early months of 1949 Poland, Czechoslovakia, Hungary, Romania, and the Soviet Union each concluded trade agreements with Albania.[1] Soviet and Eastern European technical advisers, many of whom had been withdrawn from Yugoslavia, now flocked to Albania to fill the gap created there by the expulsion of the Yugoslav specialists. The Soviet contingent, led by Minister Dimitri Chuvakin, began to exercise a commanding influence in the direction of Albanian policy.[2] Thus, by the beginning of 1949, Albania had progressed from the status of a sub-satellite to that of a full-fledged satellite of the Soviet Union.

[1] Skendi, *Albania*, pp. 231–35, 352–53.
[2] Kertesz, *The Fate of East Central Europe*, p. 312; Seton-Watson, *East-European Revolution*, p. 229.

In addition to wanting to keep Albania from falling under Yugoslav domination, the Soviet Union after 1948 also became interested in the country for strategic reasons. Albania now replaced Yugoslavia as the main base of operations and refuge for General Markos and his Greek communist guerrillas.[3] Second, the Soviet Union, which had contemplated building a naval base in Yugoslavia, now hoped to find a suitable site for it in Albania and by 1950 decided to reactivate the former Italian-Nazi submarine base on the island of Sazan, at the mouth of the Bay of Vlorë. Sazan, which lies only some 50 miles from the important Italian naval station at Otranto, would thus provide the Soviet Union with an effective center of operations to counteract Western and Yugoslav sea power in the Adriatic. It would also give the Soviets direct access to the Mediterranean Sea. By 1952 the facilities on Sazan were made operational. The Soviet government then dispatched a fleet of twelve W-class submarines along with a small flotilla of auxiliary vessels to the Vlorë-Sazan area where they took up permanent station. Between 1950 and 1960, the Soviet Union reportedly spent in excess of $30 million to develop and maintain this naval complex.[4]

In addition to the purely military factors, which were undoubtedly quite important in the early 1950s, the Soviet move into Albania was also partially motivated by psychological considerations. Albania was geographically isolated from the other members of the

[3] With the cessation of hostilities in Greece in late 1949 the military significance of the Communist bases in Albania was greatly reduced.

[4] For a discussion of Soviet naval operations in Albania during the 1950's see Leo Heiman, "Peking's Adriatic Stronghold," *East Europe*, XII, No. 4 (April 1964), pp. 15–16.

Communist Bloc. Furthermore, prior to the formation of the Warsaw Treaty Organization, Albania was not bound by a treaty of mutual assistance to the Soviet Union or any of the People's Democracies except Bulgaria. Albania's army was ill-equipped and poorly trained; her air force virtually nonexistent. The establishment of the Soviet submarine base in Albania may thus have also been designed to reassure the Albanian government and people, surrounded as they were by hostile neighbors, that they enjoyed the support and protection of the Kremlin.

As both Western and Soviet military technology improved, the strategic importance of the Sazan-Vlorë complex and of Albania itself gradually diminished. The logistical problems involved in supplying and garrisoning Albania, coupled with the growing vulnerability of Albania to attack from the West, made it impractical for the Soviets to transform Albania into a "Red Gilbraltar" on the Adriatic. Also, lack of confidence in the Albanian leaders kept the Kremlin from transforming Albania into a major base for Soviet operations in the Mediterranean Sea.

Indeed, during the early part of 1949, Enver Hoxha may have had some doubts concerning his own future as the Soviets began to consolidate their hold on Albania, for he felt impelled to make secret overtures to both the United States and Great Britain to obtain diplomatic recognition for his regime. His efforts, however, were unsuccessful.[5] Stalin, who probably had no intention of removing Hoxha from power at this critical period, then invited the Albanian dictator to Moscow in March, 1949, to sign the Soviet-Albanian trade agreement. On this occasion Stalin, perhaps sensing the

[5] Kertesz, *The Fate of East Central Europe*, pp. 311–12.

Albanian leader's uneasiness, gave his permission to Hoxha to proceed with the purge of Koçi Xoxe and his clique.[6]

Within a month of his return from Moscow Hoxha put Xoxe and his principal accomplices on trial on charges of treason. After a secret hearing in Tiranë in May, 1949, Xoxe was condemned to be shot and his co-defendents were given prison sentences.[7] The trial and execution of Xoxe triggered off a wave of "Titoist" purges in Eastern Europe during late 1949 and the early 1950s, which resulted in the liquidation of such communist stalwarts as Laszlo Rajk in Hungary and Traicho Kostov in Bulgaria.

Capitalizing upon the anti-Tito hysteria which was sweeping through the Communist Bloc, Hoxha pressed his offensive against the genuine Titoists in the Albanian Party and even widened the scope of his drive to include those individuals who opposed his policies. Before the "Titoist purge" in Albania had run its course, fourteen of the thirty-one members of the Central Committee and thirty-two of the 109 deputies of the People's Assembly would be liquidated.[8] At the Third Plenum of the Central Committee of the Albanian Party of Labor in October, 1949,[9] the Albanian dictator expressed his displeasure at the inefficiency of the state security organs in ferreting out the enemies of

[6] Wolff, *Balkans in Our Time,* p. 379.

[7] *Dokumenta Kryesore* I, pp. 484–85, n. 97.

[8] Zbigniew K. Brzezinski, *The Soviet Bloc: Unity and Conflict* (New York: Frederick A. Praeger, 1963), p. 431.

[9] For the text of the resolution of the Third Plenum of the APL, see *Dokumenta Kryesore të Partisë së Punës së Shqipërisë,* II (Principal Documents of the Albanian Party of Labor) (Tiranë: Instituti i Historisë së Partisë Pranë K.Q. të P.P. Sh., 1961) (hereafter cited as *Dokumenta Kryesore* II), pp. 15–19, doc. 61.

the state and criticized the judiciary for its leniency. He also censured the economic planners and administrators for not taking the necessary steps to eliminate the "destructive influence" of the Titoists.

In April, 1950, Hoxha convened the Second National Conference of the Albanian Party of Labor to ratify formally the decree of the Central Committee which recommended the ouster of Minister of Industry Abedin Shehu and Deputy Communications Minister Niazi Islami from their posts for "anti-party and . . . anti-Soviet activities." Abedin Shehu was also dropped from the Central Committee. In addition, the Conference was informed that the leaders of the "Abedin Shehu faction" in the army, Nexhip Vinçani and Gjin Marku, had been stripped of their commands.[10]

After the conclusion of the conference, trials of Titoist elements were staged in a number of Albanian cities including Tiranë, Durrës, and Kukës.[11] At this point, however, the Central Committee decided to abandon its piecemeal tactics and ordered a thorough housecleaning at all levels of the Party. In the summer of 1950 the members of the Albanian Party were required to surrender their credentials for re-evaluation. This action resulted in the expulsion of eight per cent of the Party membership (approximately 4,000 individuals).[12]

During 1950–51 the unrest within the country was also manifested by the fact that the cabinet was

[10] *Ibid.*, pp. 20–32, doc. 62.
[11] *Yugoslav White Book*, p. 139.
[12] Bisha, "Nga historia," p. 90. During the "Titoist purge" of the Party from November 1948 to December 1951 approximately 12,000 persons (about 25 per cent of the membership) were dropped from the rolls of the APL. *New York Times*, April 17, 1952.

reshuffled on several occasions.[13] In 1951, a new wave of purges was unleashed after a bomb was exploded in the Soviet Legation in Tiranë in February and after a series of minor skirmishes had occurred along the Albanian-Yugoslav frontier. The chief victims of these purges were Tuk Jakova, Party Secretary for Organization; Teodor Heba, the Chief of the Directory of Cadres; and Manol Konomi, Minister of Justice. In addition, the party secretaries of the Tiranë, Elbasan, and Vlorë districts lost their jobs. The deposition of these individuals provides further evidence of the breakdown in discipline in the Albanian Party following the split with Tito. Tuk Jakova, who had opposed Hoxha's policy of rapid industrialization and who did not appear to have been anxious to purge the non-Titoist opponents of Hoxha, was relieved of his position as Organizational Secretary and dropped from the Politburo. He was, however, permitted to retain his membership on the Central Committee. This latter gesture was perhaps designed to preserve a measure of unity in the Party. Konomi, who had aroused the ire of Hoxha and Minister of the Interior Mehmet Shehu for attempting to preserve a semblance of fairness in the administration of justice, was expelled from the Central Committee, as was Heba, an ally of Jakova.[14]

After the removal of Jakova and his associates, Hoxha and Shehu took personal charge of the final phase of the re-evaluation of the Party membership.

[13] During the spring of 1950, the United States and Great Britain sought to capitalize on the unrest in Albania by organizing an uprising against the communist regime. This plot was betrayed by the Soviet counterspy H. A. R. Philby and was quickly crushed by the Albanian authorities. The failure of this plan discouraged similar ventures in the party states of Eastern Europe. *Chicago Tribune,* February 28, 1968.

[14] *Dokumenta Kryesore* II, pp. 61–68, doc. 66.

Following the completion of this process in September 1951, they began to make plans for the convocation of the Second Congress of the Albanian Party of Labor, which was scheduled to meet in March 1952. Despite the fact that the Party leadership had sought to fill the vacancies caused by those who had been purged between 1949 and 1951, the overall Party membership in March 1952 was 44,418 as opposed to 45,382 in November 1948.[15]

The decisions of the Second Congress of the Albanian Party of Labor, which met between March 31 and April 7, 1952, reflected the triumph of Hoxha and the Stalinists over the Titoists and moderates. Hoxha was unanimously re-elected Party Secretary. The Party condemned Titoism and right wing deviationism, reaffirmed its support of the program of rapid industrialization, and called for an intensive drive to popularize collectivization of agriculture. The Congress approved Hoxha's plan to broaden the base of the Party by admitting more workers, who in 1952 comprised only 11.5 per cent of its membership, into its ranks. It also placed itself on record as recognizing the need for improving the ideological level and organization of the Party. The economic assistance of the Soviet Union was gratefully acknowledged and the Party agreed to strive to improve relations with the U.S.S.R. and the communist states of Eastern Europe.[16]

During the year between the Second Party Congress and the death of Stalin, Hoxha and his clique suc-

[15] *Ibid.*, pp. 252–53, doc. 78. The thoroughness of the purges of the post-Tito period is evidenced by the fact that of the 44,418 Albanian communists in 1952 only 29,932 were full members of the Party and 14,486 were classified as candidates.

[16] For the proceedings of the Second Congress of the Albanian Party of Labor see *ibid.*, pp. 129–74, docs. 71, 72.

ceeded in consolidating their position in Albania. By early 1953, on the eve of Stalin's death, it appeared that political conditions in Albania had finally stabilized. The Albanian leaders were firmly committed to the policies of the Soviet Union, which at this time closely paralleled their own. Hoxha was sincerely dedicated to the proposition of transforming Albania into a socialist state patterned after the Soviet model.

This desire was most clearly manifested in the economic sphere. The foundations for the establishment of a planned economy were laid by forming an Economic and Planning Commission in 1945 and 1946.[17] Between 1946 and 1949 the state refined the planning system to assure more effective central control of the economy. The Soviet cost accounting system (*khozraschet*) was introduced in 1947. A year later the State Bank was designated as the sole agency for the conduct of transactions between government enterprises. This action provided the state with an efficient weapon for regulating the various sectors of the nation's economy. Adequate capital to finance economic development was secured by the creation of a savings bank system in 1948 and by forcing the people to subscribe to government loans. In 1949, following the example of other Eastern European states, Albania adopted the essential features of the Soviet fiscal system. Direct taxes were drastically reduced and indirect levies were compounded into a turnover tax. Under this arrangement state enterprises made direct contributions to the treasury from their profits and retained only that share authorized for self-financed investments and other purposes. The Ministry of Finance thus had the power to determine the investment policy of each state enter-

[17] *ESE*, 1960, chap. vi, p. 5.

prise and through the State Bank to supervise and regulate, if necessary, its current activity.[18] While these innovations would not be perfected for several years, they nevertheless did make it possible for Albania to embark upon a program of planned economic development.

In fact, Albania had adopted its first economic plan, the Nine Month Plan for 1947, even before the reorganization of the economy had been completed. This plan was essentially a series of investment allocations. A substantial portion of the 1,539 million leks ($30,-780,000) budgeted to finance this plan was earmarked for the construction of the 43 kilometer Durrës-Peqin railroad and other public works projects. Of the remaining funds, 25 per cent was allocated for industry and mining and the rest was used to finance agricultural and social welfare improvements.

One year later, a more ambitious plan provided for a more extensive outlay of investment funds for development purposes and established production goals for certain commodities such as copper, coal, oil, bitumen, textiles, and building materials, but it failed to meet its objectives owing to the Yugoslav-Albanian split.[19]

After the break with Tito the Albanian government initiated a Two-Year Plan for 1949–50 with an investment outlay of 4,147,000,000 leks ($82,940,000). This plan was more comprehensive than those of 1947 and 1948, its investment allocations were more detailed, and its production targets were broadened to include a larger segment of the industrial and mining sectors of the economy as well as agriculture. This Two-Year Plan, however, fell short of its goals because a shortage of capital necessitated a cutback of 20 per cent in the

[18] Ibid., pp. 7–8; Skendi, Albania, pp. 219–223.
[19] ESE, 1960, chap. vi, p. 6; Skendi, Albania, p. 191.

projected investments for industry. Consequently, while the average rate of industrial growth for the years 1949–50 was 10.5 per cent, the planned targets for industry and mining were only 78.6 and 74.1 per cent fulfilled. The results were similarly disappointing in agriculture where farm output rose an average of only 2.1 per cent. The government found it especially difficult to enforce its agricultural directives, since 94 per cent of the farm production was derived from the private sector of the economy. The shortcomings of the Two-Year Plan, which the Albanian regime said had been only 87.2 per cent fulfilled, were attributed largely to the indifference and hostility of the deposed Minister of Industry Abedin Shehu and the influence of the Titoists.[20]

During the period of short-term planning, the efforts of the Albanian regime were primarily designed to repair, improve, and expand the transportation and communications network and to increase the amount of land under cultivation. By 1950, however, the emphasis in investment had shifted to industry, which now received almost 50 per cent of the state development funds, while only 25 per cent was allotted for public works. Although state investment in agriculture had tripled between 1945 and 1950, it had declined as a percentage of the total from 21.3 to 9.8 during this period.[21]

Having gained the requisite experience in the planning and control of the economy, the Albanian government inaugurated its First Five-Year Plan (1951–55)

[20] For details of the Two Year Plan see *Dokumenta Kryesore* II, pp. 69–77, doc. 67; pp. 148–49, doc. 71; Skendi, *Albania*, pp. 177–78, 191, 194, 198, 201, 245, 252, 256, 264; Wolff, *Balkans in Our Time*, pp. 541–42.

[21] *ESE*, 1960, chap. vi, pp. 6–7.

in January, 1951. The Plan, which allocated approximately 43 per cent of its budget of 21 billion leks ($420,000,000) for industrial development, reflected the desire of the leadership of the Albanian Party to create "the technical-material basis" for the building of socialism in Albania by transforming the country from an agricultural nation to an agricultural-industrial nation. Primary emphasis was placed on the exploitation of the country's mineral resources, especially chrome, copper, nickel, oil, asphalt, and coal; the electrification of the nation; and the expansion of light and food processing industries. According to the Plan, the average annual rate of industrial growth was projected at 27.7 per cent. It was expected that the output of heavy industry would rise 31 per cent and that of light industry 26.5 per cent each year.[22]

In agriculture the First Five-Year Plan called for an increase of 71 per cent in gross farm output. The government hoped to achieve this objective by speeding up the tempo of collectivization, mechanizing and modernizing agricultural techniques, and increasing the area under cultivation. In April, 1951, the Central Committee approved a proposal to institute a program of rapid and forced collectivization. A month later, however, the same body meeting in special session reversed this decision owing to widespread peasant opposition. Between 1951 and 1953, therefore, the Albanian regime concentrated its efforts in the areas of agricultural mechanization and land reclamation. In the latter category the government hoped to utilize the vast reservoir of manpower at its disposal to minimize the need for capital investment.[23]

[22] *Dokumenta Kryesore* II, pp. 105–109, doc. 69; p. 154, doc. 72; p. 162, doc. 72.
[23] *Ibid.*, pp. 79–101, doc. 68; *ESE*, 1960, chap. vi, pp. 6–9.

Although the proposed expenditures for the improvement of transportation and communication facilities under the First Five-Year Plan amounted to only 16 per cent of the total outlay, the Albanian leaders nevertheless hoped to make rapid progress in highway and railroad construction by the use of "voluntary" and convict labor. The Albanian planners foresaw the addition of 300 kilometers to the existing highway system and the modernization of another 140 kilometers of existing roadways. The Durrës-Peqin railroad line was to be expanded by the construction of new branches from Durrës to Tiranë and from Peqin to Elbasan. In addition, the Plan provided for the construction of a 90-kilometer line from the coal fields at Memaliaj to Vlorë and a seven-kilometer spur to the Çerrik oil refinery. The Plan also called for the improvement of the harbor and dock facilities at Durrës, Albania's principal port.[24]

The success of the First Five-Year Plan was, of course, contingent upon the assistance of the Soviet Union and the People's Democracies. This fact is best illustrated by an examination of the Albanian balance of payments for the years 1951–53, which show an average annual deficit of $26,100,000. This deficit was underwritten by the U.S.S.R. and the other communist states in the form of long-term grants, which were in effect subsidies, since there was little likelihood that Albania would be able to pay them in the foreseeable future. Albania, whose trade was conducted almost exclusively within the communist bloc during the First Five-Year Plan, imported industrial and agricultural machinery, chemicals, building materials, textiles, and consumer goods while she exported crude oil, chrome

[24] Skendi, *Albania*, pp. 242–48.

and copper ores, bitumen, wood products, hides and skins, and foodstuffs.[25]

As in its dealings with other communist states, the Soviet Union sought to derive the maximum advantage from its commercial relations with Albania. The U.S.S.R. was anxious to exploit Albania's mineral resources but was less inclined to help the country construct its own refining or processing plants. Albania thus exported sizable quantities of mineral raw materials but was required to import processed oil and metal products. Under these circumstances Albania found herself falling deeper and deeper into the debt of the Eastern European satellites and the Soviet Union, since her raw material exports brought only a small return compared to the prices she had to pay for finished or refined imports.

Between 1949 and 1953, the state embarked upon a planned development program while it attempted simultaneously to transform the social and cultural life of Albania. The objectives of the regime were to improve the health and intellectual-technical capacities of the population in order to provide the state with the requisite work force, and to eliminate those institutions, traditions, attitudes, and ideologies which still posed threats to the creation of a communist state in Albania.

During the immediate post-war era, a modest campaign was financed by U.N.R.R.A., to improve the health and sanitation conditions in the country. This program sought to increase the number of professionally trained medical personnel, expand hospital facilities, reduce the incidence of such endemic diseases as malaria, and improve housing conditions. By

[25] For an analysis of Albanian foreign trade for 1951–53 see *ESE*, 1960, chap. vi, p. 13; Skendi, *Albania*, pp. 232–36.

101

1953 some progress toward achieving these objectives was recorded. The number of physicians had risen from 110 to about 150, a three-year school for the preparation of medical assistants had been created, a medical college was established in Tiranë, and eighty-four Albanians received degrees in medicine, dentistry, and pharmacy from Soviet and Eastern European institutions of higher learning.

Hospital facilities also increased from fourteen hospitals with a bed capacity of 1,765 in the entire nation in 1945 to over 100 health institutions of various types with a capacity of about 5,500 beds in 1953.[26]

Spraying and draining of marsh lands reduced the incidence of malaria among the Albanian population from 70 per cent in 1945–46 to 7.7 per cent in 1953, and gains were also scored against tuberculosis and syphilis.[27]

The achievements of the Albanian government in improving housing and sanitation during these years were not especially impressive. Approximately 10 per cent of the First Five-Year Plan's investment outlay ($41,880,000) was allocated for the construction of new housing and sanitary facilities, but most of this money was spent in the urban industrialized centers and not in the rural areas where the need was greatest. Another factor which undermined the government health campaign was the chronic food shortage that plagued Albania during the late 1940s and early 1950s.[28]

Despite these shortcomings, however, the general

[26] *Anuari Statistikor, 1961*, pp. 268; *Vjetari Statistikor i R.P. Sh., 1963* ("Statistical Yearbook of the A[lbanian] P[eople's] R[epublic], 1963") (hereafter cited as *Vjetari Statistikor, 1963*) (Tiranë: Drejtoria e Statistikës, 1964), pp. 347, 356. The figures for 1953 are estimates.

[27] Skendi, *Albania*, p. 260.

[28] *Ibid.*, pp. 256–58.

health of the Albanian people does appear to have improved somewhat by 1953, when the death rate declined from 16.7 to 13.6 per 1000, and the infant mortality rate dropped from 112.2 to 99.5 per 1000.[29]

The period from 1949 to 1953 also witnessed improvement in the Albanian educational system, the objectives of which were the propagation of communist ideology and providing the academic and technical training necessary for the construction of a socialist state and society. The Hoxha regime had launched a drive against illiteracy in 1946, and by the time the first phase of this project was completed in 1950, the illiteracy rate had fallen from 60 per cent to 31 per cent.[30] At the same time, the school system was reorganized along Soviet lines. In addition, the government established five institutions on the secondary level to train teachers for service in the primary and seven-year schools and a two-year teachers' college to provide faculty for the secondary schools.[31]

By 1950, the number of schools, pupils, and teachers had doubled in comparison with the total for each of these categories in 1945.[32] In October, 1950, the scope of the educational system was expanded with secondary vocational schools (teknikums) to train personnel in such areas as health services, business, finance, and agriculture. The following year, three "higher institutes" offering four year programs in education, engineering, and agriculture for secondary school graduates

[29] *Anuari Statistikor, 1961*, p. 57.

[30] *Dokumenta Kryesore* II, p. 151, doc. 71; *Vjetari Statistikor, 1963*, p. 61.

[31] Skendi, *Albania*, pp. 278–79.

[32] Between 1945 and 1950, the number of schools in Albania rose from 1122 to 2222, student enrollment increased from 84,746 to 172,831, and the teaching staff grew from 2281 to 4942. *Anuari Statistikor, 1961*, p. 251.

were established. In 1952, two additional "higher institutes" of medicine and economics began operation. There were no universities in Albania and the government was obliged to send students abroad for advanced professional training. Between 1949 and 1953, 671 Albanian students received degrees from foreign universities, mainly in the Soviet Union. The largest number of degrees were earned in engineering, with agriculture, medicine, and economics following in that order.[33]

Development of the educational system was regarded by the government as a key factor in changing Albania into a socialist state and 3.46 billion leks ($69,200,000) were budgeted for this purpose in the First Five-Year Plan. The Soviet Union provided scholarships for Albanian students studying abroad and supplied Albania with specialists and materials to improve instruction at home,[34] with the aim of transforming Albanian youth into dedicated communists and strong partisans of the Soviet Union.

After pursuing a rather moderate policy toward the three major religious bodies in Albania in the immediate post war era, the government reversed its tactics during the years between the break with Tito and the death of Stalin.[35] The loosely organized muslim community fell under the control of the state with the appointment of the pro-communist Hafiz Musa Haxhi Ali as head of the non-Bektashi Albanian muslim groups, while the Bektashis became subservient when

[33] Skendi, *Albania*, pp. 279–80; *Anuari Statistikor, 1961*, p. 268.

[34] Skendi, *Albania*, pp. 281–84 *passim.*

[35] For religious developments in Albania during this period see Skendi, *Albania*, pp. 293–99; Wolff, *Balkans in Our Time*, pp. 556, 563–64, 567–68.

a prominent wartime pro-communist resistance leader, Mustafa Faja Marteneshi, was elevated to the post of Bektashi Chief Grandfather. Faja was assassinated in 1947 and Ahmed Myfta Dede, also sympathetic to the communists, became leader of the Bektashis. The state discouraged instruction in the Islamic faith and attendance at religious services, and as the number of practicing muslims began to decline, the government closed down or razed many mosques. By the early 1950s the influence of Islam was in decline and the muslim community did not pose a serious threat to the communists.

The communists made no serious effort to interfere with the Orthodox Church until August, 1949, when they deposed Archbishop Kristofor Kisi, Primate of the Church of Albania, who had opposed their attempts to use the church as a vehicle for communist propaganda. Kisi was replaced by Bishop Pashko Vodica (Paisi) of Korçë, an ardent supporter of the communists during World War II. Paisi secured a new charter for the Albanian Orthodox Church, which was to develop a sense of loyalty to the regime among the orthodox faithful of Albania. During the early 1950s the Albanian Orthodox Church strengthened its ties with the Patriarchate of Moscow, purged from its ranks those clergymen who were not sympathetic to the communists, and became for all practical purposes a tool of the Albanian government.

Although the Catholic Church was the smallest of the religious bodies in Albania, it suffered the greatest at the hands of the communists for several reasons. The catholics—especially some members of the clergy— had tended to collaborate with the Nazis and Italians during the occupation; they maintained ties with the Vatican; and they were concentrated in northern Al-

105

bania where the opposition to the Tiranë government was greatest. Between 1945 and 1949, the communists had sought to discredit the Catholic Church by expelling the Papal Nuncio and imprisoning a number of prominent catholic clergymen. The independence of the Catholic Church was finally destroyed in 1951, when a new constitution for the Catholic Church of Albania in effect nationalized the church. It prohibited direct relations with the Vatican. The state assumed control of all seminaries, agreed to subsidize the church, and appointed an aged Franciscan friar, Msgr. Bernardin Shallaku, as spiritual leader of the Albanian catholic community. By 1953, the influence of the Catholic Church had greatly diminished. Many of its churches were closed, while only 22 of the 187 members of the clergy were still at liberty, and their activities were subject to strict regulation.

Between 1949 and 1953 Albania was too deeply engrossed with her own problems to play a significant role in the affairs of the communist camp. In foreign affairs the Albanians were more concerned with the threats posed to their security by Yugoslavia and Greece than with matters of general interest to the communist states of Eastern Europe. Albania was much too weak and dependent on the Soviet Union to adopt a posture other than that of unswerving obedience to the Kremlin.

Of primary concern to the Albanians were their relations with the Yugoslavs. The Albanian-Yugoslav split had resulted in the outbreak of a violent propaganda campaign between the two nations. Tiranë accused Belgrade of mistreating and seeking to exterminate the Albanian population of Kosovo and of scheming to promote a rebellion in Northern Albania against the Hoxha regime.[36] The Yugoslavs in turn took the Albanians to task for restricting the movements of their diplomatic mission in Tiranë and for attempting to stir up trouble among the Kosovars. During the Titoist purge trials in 1949, Yugoslavia repudiated its Treaty of Friendship and Mutual Assistance with Albania.[37]

In May, 1950, the Yugoslavs withdrew their diplomatic mission from Tiranë in retaliation for the harassment to which it had been subjected there. In November, the Albanian Legation in Belgrade was closed on orders from Tito,[38] but diplomatic relations between the two states had merely been suspended, not formally broken at this time.

Hoping to capitalize upon the unrest which existed in Albania, the Yugoslav government convoked a congress of Albanian political exiles and Kosovars at Prizren in May, 1951. The Congress called for the creation of an "independent democratic Albania" and urged the Albanian people to rise up against the Hoxha dictatorship. The Yugoslavs at this time also tried to organize an Albanian Communist Party in exile, but they soon abandoned this project owing to a lack of support from the Albanians in Yugoslavia.[39]

Hoxha was now alarmed at the developments in Yugoslavia, and he sought a firm commitment of assistance from the Soviet Union in the event that Belgrade decided to launch a new venture in Albania. The Albanian dictator could not have been unmindful

---

[36] For a sampling of anti-Yugoslav propaganda see *Yugoslav White Book*, pp. 256–59, docs. 132–37; pp. 386–93, docs. 247–253.

[37] *New York Times*, November 13, 1949.

[38] Saikowski, "Albania in Soviet Satellite Policy," p. 29.

[39] *Lufta P.P. Sh. kundër LKJ*, p. 53.

of the lowly position which his country occupied in the Soviet bloc. With the exception of East Germany, Albania was the only satellite state which by 1952 did not possess a treaty of mutual assistance with the Soviet Union. Soviet-Albanian relations were still conducted at the ministerial level. After the formation of COMECON, not one of the permanent committees of the organization had chosen to make its headquarters in Tiranë.

The Soviet government was not unaware of the fears of the Albanians. In 1950, Moscow dispatched a 480-man military mission to Albania to help train the armed forces and also provided the Albanians with relatively modern arms. A 200-man Bulgarian military mission was also sent to instruct the Albanian army in guerrilla warfare techniques.[40] These gestures, however, do not appear to have completely satisfied the Albanians.

To further bolster the morale of the Albanian people, all the party states of Europe and Asia sent representatives to Albania in November, 1952, to celebrate the eighth anniversary of the liberation of the country from Axis rule and the fortieth anniversary of Albanian independence. Never before had such as assemblage of communist dignitaries been present at one time on Albanian soil. Mehmet Shehu on this occasion sought to elicit from the Soviet Union a specific pledge that the U.S.S.R. would come to the aid of Albania if she were attacked by a foreign power.[41] Moscow, however, remained noncommittal on this matter.

Thus, when on February 28, 1953, Greece, Turkey, and Yugoslavia signed a Treaty of Friendship and

[40] Saikowski, "Albania in Soviet Satellite Policy," p. 36.
[41] Radio Tiranë, November 28, 1952.

Collaboration, Tiranë interpreted this act as a move to prepare the way for the partition of Albania. Hoxha sought to rally public support for his regime by raising the specter of foreign intervention in Albania and depicting himself as the only individual capable of preserving the independence and integrity of the nation.[42] Before the Albanian leader could appeal to the Soviet Union for direct aid, the world was informed on March 5, 1953, of the death of Joseph Stalin. The death of Stalin and the resulting shift in the course of Soviet foreign policy in the post-Stalin era were to have a profound effect upon Soviet-Albanian relations.

[42] *Dokumenta Kryesore* II, p. 269, doc. 78.

4: THE THAW AND THE APPROACHING SCHISM WITH THE U.S.S.R., 1953-60

The death of Stalin in March, 1953, which occurred at the point when the leaders of the Albanian Party of Labor had just succeeded in consolidating their hold on the nation and Party following the Titoist purges, caused much consternation in Tiranë. Hoxha and Shehu could not help but wonder what the future would hold in store for them as a result of the changes that were taking place in the Soviet Union since the passing of the Soviet dictator. Furthermore, there was also a danger that dissident elements within Albania might take advantage of the new situation created by Stalin's death to launch a rebellion against the government. For this reason neither Hoxha nor Shehu went to Moscow to pay their last respects to Stalin. Albania on this occasion was represented by second-rank Party functionaries such as Abdyl Kellezi, Minister of Finance, and by General Beqir Balluku and Liri Belishova, both of whom were then studying in Moscow.[1]

The impact of Stalin's death was soon felt in Albania. In July, 1953, Albania, following the example of the Soviet Union and the other satellite states, took a first step toward implementing the new policy of collective leadership. Hoxha relinquished his posts as Foreign and Defense Minister while still retaining

[1] Skendi, *Albania*, pp. 324-25, 331.

111

those of Party Secretary and Prime Minister. The Cabinet at this time was reduced in size from nineteen to ten when the functions of several ministries were combined. There were also a few major changes within the Party, the most notable of which was the removal of Shehu from his post as Secretary of the Secretariat of the APL.[2]

During the summer of 1953, Albania's relations with Greece and Turkey remained tense despite the declaration of the foreign ministers of the Balkan Pact signatories that "the independence of Albania would constitute an important element for the peace and stability of the Balkans."[3] On August 2, in a speech before the People's Assembly, Hoxha renewed his attacks upon the Balkan Pact by branding it as "an instrument of aggression." He reiterated his previous charge that its major purpose was to seek the dismemberment of Albania.[4] Two days later, in an article which appeared in *Pravda*, the Soviet government warned that any attempt on the part of the Balkan Pact signatories to strengthen their relations with NATO would be viewed as a "threat to the immediate neighbors of Greece, Turkey, and Yugoslavia and in particular to Albania."

In August, 1953, the Albanian and Soviet governments announced that their diplomatic relations would henceforth be conducted at the ambassadorial level.[5] This gesture was probably designed to raise the prestige of the Albanian leaders and to boost the morale of the Albanian people.

[2] *New York Times*, July 25, 1953; Skendi, *Albania*, p. 343. Shehu kept his post as Minister of the Interior.

[3] *New York Times*, July 12, 1953.

[4] Radio Tiranë, August 2, 1953.

[5] Skendi, *Albania*, p. 350.

As Soviet-Yugoslav relations began to improve during the summer and fall of 1953, Moscow applied pressure upon Tiranë to effect a rapprochement with Belgrade, and on December 22, 1953, Albania and Yugoslavia resumed diplomatic relations, which had been suspended in 1950.[6]

Although the Albanian government was growing increasingly apprehensive over developments in the communist camp and in the Balkans during 1953, it was forced to devote greater attention to domestic problems when it became evident that serious difficulties had arisen in the nation's economy. In the Central Committee session in December, 1953, Enver Hoxha noted the serious weakness of the Albanian economy in the agricultural sector, caused by too large a proportion of the assistance from the Soviet Union and the People's Democracies having been used for industrial development while agriculture was being ignored. He took the economic planners to task for failing to take proper measures to ensure that the Plan was being fulfilled and for having approved a Plan that was not "rational."[7]

The Central Committee ordered a drastic cutback in the industrial construction program. To stimulate agricultural production, delivery quotas for grain, meat, and wool were reduced; peasants and cooperatives were relieved of paying their tax arrears for 1953; and additional financial and technical aid was promised for agriculture.[8]

The revised economic program approved by the

[6] *Ibid.*, p. 29.

[7] *Dokumenta Kryesore* II, pp. 300–304, doc. 80.

[8] *Ibid.*, pp. 304–9; *Mbi kontradiktat* (Concerning Contradictions) (Tiranë: N. Sh. Botimeve "Naim Frashëri," 1962), pp. 97–99.

Central Committee in December, 1953, closely paralleled that of the "New Course" which was associated with the rise of Malenkov to power in the Soviet Union. The new Albanian economic policies were probably inspired both by pressures from Moscow as well as by conditions in Albania.

It was obvious by the end of 1953 that Albania could not fulfill the goals set for industrial development under the First Five-Year Plan. The planned reduction of foreign aid for 1954 must have also convinced the Albanian leaders of the need to overhaul their economic policies.

The year 1954 saw several important developments take place both in the political and economic spheres. In July, a second significant step in the direction of collective leadership was taken when Hoxha gave up the Prime Ministry and Mehmet Shehu now became Prime Minister. Although Hoxha's power was diminished, he retained the leading position in the Party, with the title of First Secretary of the Central Committee.[9] These moves at least created the impression that the principle of collective leadership was being practiced in Albania.

While the Albanian leaders outwardly accepted the new Soviet line, there appears to have been some behind-the-scenes concern in Tiranë, caused by the reduction in foreign aid and by the gradual thawing of Moscow–Belgrade relations. Taking advantage of the Soviet Union's somewhat relaxed grip on the satellite states, Hoxha and Shehu began to look about the communist bloc for an additional source of aid.

[9] *New York Times*, July 21, 1954. See also Enver Hoxha, *Rapport d'activité du Comité Central du Parti du Travail d'Albanie au IIIe Congrès du Parti* (Tiranë: Enterprise d'Editions de l'Etat, 1956), pp. 186–87.

They found one in China. In October, 1954, Tiranë
and Peking signed a series of agreements providing for
cultural, scientific, and technical cooperation.[10] In December of the same year their relations were further
cemented when China presented Albania with a gift
of approximately two and one half million dollars
worth of commodities of various types and a loan of
twelve and one half million dollars for the years 1955–
1960.[11] These new sources of aid helped in part to
mitigate the adverse effect of the cutback in economic
support from the European communist states. The
Albanian-Chinese Agreements in 1954 also marked the
first step in the formation of the Sino-Albanian entente.

In late November, 1954, the suspicions which Hoxha
and Shehu harbored toward the new Soviet leaders
were somewhat lessened when Albania was invited to
a conference in Moscow, called by the Soviet government in the wake of the decision of the NATO powers
to admit the Federal Republic of Germany into that
organization and to permit her to re-arm. The Albanian government endorsed the decision of the conference to form a rival collective security organization
in Eastern Europe when and if the West Germans
agreed to enter NATO. On May 14, 1955, shortly after
the Federal Republic of Germany had become a member of NATO, the communist states of Europe met in
Warsaw where they created the Warsaw Treaty Organization. Albania was a charter member of this group.
Insofar as Albania was concerned, this action was of

[10] Skendi, *Albania*, p. 352.
[11] Colin Garratt, "China as a Foreign Aid Donor," *China:
The Emerging Red Giant: Communist Foreign Policies*, ed.
Devere E. Pentony (San Francisco: Chandler Publishing Com-
pany, 1962), pp. 202–3; Jan S. Prybyla, "Albania's Economic
Vassalage," *East Europe*, XVIII, No. 1 (January 1967), p. 10.

special significance, since it meant that the security of that nation was now guaranteed by the Soviet Union and the Eastern European satellites.[12] The conclusion of the Warsaw Pact marked the first occasion on which the Soviet Union and the People's Democracies had committed themselves to come to the assistance of Albania should she be a victim of foreign aggression.

During the spring of 1955, as Soviet-Yugoslav relations continued to improve, Hoxha and Shehu once again feared that a Soviet-Yugoslav rapprochement might well result in their removal from power. If we are to believe the official Albanian accounts, such an attempt was made at a meeting of the Central Committee in April, 1955, by Tuk Jakova and Bedri Spahiu, but Hoxha prevailed while Jakova and Spahiu were "relieved" of all "official duties."[13]

This move, coming only a month after the Khrushchev-Bulganin visit to Belgrade, represented Hoxha's initial reaction to the Soviet-Yugoslav rapprochement.

In their denunciation of Jakova and Spahiu, Hoxha and the Central Committee had taken pains not to brand them as Titoists or pro-Yugoslavs. Their caution about not offending Moscow paid off when it became evident that the Kremlin expected Albania and the other bloc states to terminate their anti-Tito campaign. Tiranë was able to comply without too much difficulty. By the late summer of 1955, the Albanian press was again printing articles recalling the close cooperation between the Albanians and the Yugoslavs during World War II. The differences which had arisen between the two nations, especially after 1948, were now attributed to the machinations of Beria.

In 1956, a Yugoslav-Albanian "thaw" was in the

[12] *Dokumenta Kryesore* II, pp. 550–51, n. 34.
[13] *Ibid.*, pp. 415–19, doc. 86.

making, but as far as the Albanians were concerned, it was nothing more than an uneasy truce. It came to an end in the early spring when Belgrade failed to respond favorably to Albanian diplomatic overtures, and when the Yugoslav press and radio intensified their criticisms of the Hoxha-Shehu regime.[14]

In addition to attempting to improve relations with Yugoslavia, Hoxha and Shehu initiated a modest internal reform program, patterned after those that had been introduced in the Soviet Union and the People's Democracies, in an effort to gain the support of the rural population for the new drive launched in December, 1955, to collectivize agriculture.[15] Between the latter part of 1955 and early 1956, the Albanian authorities also reduced the power of the secret police, encouraged freer discussion within the Party, and even minimized somewhat the role of the Party in certain areas of Albanian life.[16]

Meanwhile, the Twentieth Congress of the CPSU met in Moscow in mid-February, 1956. The policy pronouncements which came from Moscow on this occasion had a tremendous impact in Albania, where they emboldened the small and hitherto silent anti-Hoxha faction of the APL to become more outspoken in its criticism of government and party policies.

From the fragmentary evidence which is currently available[17] it appears that the opponents of the Hoxha-

[14] *Lufta P.P.Sh. kundër LKJ*, pp. 61–63.

[15] *Dokumenta Kryesore* II, pp. 453–57, doc. 91; pp. 438–41, doc. 89.

[16] Hamm, *Albania—China's Beachhead*, p. 100. It was also at this time (December 1955) that Albania was admitted into the United Nations as part of the package deal engineered by the Soviet Union and the United States.

[17] For summary accounts of the April 1956 Tiranë city Party conference, see Hoxha, *Rapport au IIIe Congrès*, pp. 190–95;

Shehu regime, led by Tuk Jakova, General Pana-
jot Plaku, General Dalli Ndreu and his wife, Liri
Gega, with the active support of the Yugoslavs and the
tacit approval of the Soviets, initiated a movement to
gain control of the Party during the spring of 1956.
They made their first bid for power in April at the
conference of the Party organization of Tiranë city.
At this meeting the dissidents criticized the Party
leadership for displaying a negative attitude toward
the masses, using undemocratic procedures to remain
in power, pursuing ill-conceived and unrealistic economic policies, failing to implement the principle of
collective leadership, and refusing to effect a genuine
rapprochement with Yugoslavia. Some delegates demanded detailed information concerning the purges
which had taken place since 1949, others called for
the rehabilitation of a number of prominent communists (including Xoxe) who had been executed or removed from power. When the meeting threatened to
get out of hand, Hoxha appeared and was able to restore order and regain control. Afterwards the Albanian Party chief acted quickly and ruthlessly. Most of
those persons who had spoken out against the leadership of the Party were severely disciplined.

A limited amount of intellectual ferment in the nation was also manifested in May, 1956, when the Albanian literary review *Nëndori* (November) printed
an article by Razi Brahimi, one of the country's most
influential literary critics, in which the author lashed
out against the tendency in communist circles to view

---

*Le procès contre le complot organisé pour liquider la Ré-
publique Populaire d'Albanie* (Tiranë: n.p., 1961), pp. 43–45,
240–41; *Lufta P.P.Sh. kundër LKJ*, pp. 64–65; Griffith, *Albania*,
pp. 24–26; *Zëri i Popullit* ("Voice of the People"), November
8, 1961; January 9, 1962.

man as a member of a class rather than as an individual. This essay decried the impersonality of communist society, and was undoubtedly influenced, as its sources would indicate, by the writings of Soviet and East European authors of the post-Stalinist thaw. Since the number of intellectuals in Albania in 1956 was quite small, and since the intellectuals for the most part were largely identified with the ruling elite, they did not pose a threat to the established order.

Besides the internal pressures during the spring of 1956, the Albanian leaders faced a Soviet demand for the rehabilitation of Xoxe. This request was conveyed to Hoxha and Shehu by two special emissaries of the Kremlin, Mikhail Suslov and Petr Pospelov, on the eve of the Third Congress of the APL. The dominant faction in the Albanian Party, however, refused to accede to the Soviet proposals.[18]

It was against this background that the Third Congress of the Albanian Party of Labor met in Tiranë between May 25 and June 3, 1956. Prior to the opening of the Congress Hoxha had hastily convened an extraordinary session of the Central Committee on May 10–11, to discuss the actions he had taken against the Party dissidents and to whip any remaining dissenters into line. The Central Committee endorsed the policies of the Party leadership and gave Hoxha a vote of confidence.[19]

In his speech to the Party Congress Hoxha reaffirmed his support of the decisions of the Twentieth Congress of the CPSU.[20] He pointed out that the Central Com-

---

[18] *Zëri i Popullit.*, January 9, 1962.

[19] *Dokumenta Kryesore* II, p. 481, doc. 97; Hoxha, *Rapport au IIIe Congrès*, p. 195.

[20] For the text of the Hoxha speech see Hoxha, *Rapport au IIIe Congrès*.

mittee of the APL had detected the cult of personality in Albania as early as July, 1954, had taken measures to eliminate this pernicious practice, and had implemented the policy of collective leadership. Hoxha also indicated that he subscribed to the Twentieth Congress doctrines of peaceful coexistence and of different roads in the building of socialism.

The Albania dictator, undoubtedly at the insistence of Moscow, admitted that, since 1948, the APL had been deceived in the formulation of its policy toward the Yugoslavs by the activities of "the filthy agent of imperialism, Beria." Having recognized their past errors, however, the Albanians now pledged to work to improve relations with Belgrade at both the state and Party levels. Hoxha indicated that he had been "persuaded" that the Yugoslavs felt the same way as he did about this matter, but his careful choice of words and his failure to mention even once the name of Tito indicated that he was not overly enthusiastic about normalizing relations with Belgrade.

On one point the Albanians remained adamant. Despite the repeated urging of the Soviet representatives, they refused to rehabilitate Koçi Xoxe, the major victim of the Titoist purges in Albania.

Despite this one major reservation, the Third Congress had formally affirmed its support of the foreign and domestic policies of the Twentieth Congress of the CPSU. Hoxha, who had crushed his opposition at home and mended his fences with the Soviet leadership, was re-elected First Secretary of the Central Committee. The Central Committee elected by the Third Congress was comprised largely of Stalinists and was completely loyal to Hoxha and Shehu. This fact and the weakness of the anti-Stalinist element in the Albanian Party rendered it unlikely that the Albanian regime would inaugurate an extensive liberalization program or effect a genuine rapprochement with Yugoslavia.

During the Third Congress of the APL, Hoxha announced that the First Five-Year Plan had been successfully concluded, overlooking the fact that the gross farm output increased by only 37 per cent instead of the planned 71 per cent, while the average annual rate of growth in industry was 22.8 per cent in contrast to the projected 27.7 per cent.[21] Some significant gains were nevertheless recorded. Real wages of industrial workers had increased by 20 per cent, per capita farm income was up by 35 per cent, and national income had risen by 70 per cent. Hoxha also announced, perhaps prematurely, that as of the end of 1955 there were no illiterate adults under the age of forty in Albania and that the number of students enrolled in the nation's schools in 1955 stood at 191,600 as opposed to the 1950 figure of 175,500.[22]

Hoxha then proposed the Second Five-Year Plan (1956–1960), which called for the investment of 21.9 billion leks ($438,000,000) in the Albanian economy, with 80.4 per cent allocated for "capital construction" and 19.6 per cent for "non-capital construction." The Plan aimed at the rapid development of industry and mining, an increase of agricultural production, and raising the standard of living and cultural level of the people. The draft proposed an average annual growth rate of 14 per cent, with the 1960 industrial production 92 per cent greater than in 1955, and with less specific but again rather ambitious collectivization targets set for agriculture.[23]

[21] *ESE*, 1960, chap. vi, p. 9. *Dokumenta Kryesore* II, p. 154, doc. 72; p. 483; doc. 98.

[22] *Ibid.*, p. 484, doc. 98.

[23] *Ibid.*, pp. 513–15, doc. 98; p. 486, doc. 98; p. 487, doc. 98; pp. 500–509, doc. 98.

Albanian-Yugoslav relations remained tense owing to the unwillingness of Tiranë to rehabilitate Xoxe. Within Albania, however, Hoxha and Shehu had so completely reasserted their authority that the former felt confident enough to travel to Peking to attend the Eighth Congress of the Chinese Communist Party. While he was in China, Hoxha probably made known to the Chinese leaders his misgivings concerning the Yugoslav policy of the Soviet Union. He apparently was encouraged by Peking's views on this matter, and upon his return to Albania he issued a statement lavishly praising the Chinese for their accomplishments and for the aid they had given the Albanians.[24] Hoxha's overtures to Peking were to pay handsome dividends, especially after the Polish and Hungarian uprisings and the subsequent reversal of Chinese foreign and domestic policies during the second half of 1957.

Of all the European communist states, Albania reacted most violently to the disturbances that occurred in Poland and Hungary in October and November, 1956. The Albanian view concerning these events was expressed by Enver Hoxha in an article he wrote in *Pravda* on November 8, 1956, to commemorate the fifteenth anniversary of the founding of the Albanian Communist Party. He recounted the difficulties which had confronted the Albanian communists in their struggle to build socialism, noted that they had been able to succeed only because they had not deviated from the example set by the Soviet Union, and, lashing out against his arch enemy Tito, castigated those "elements who want to lure communists and the people [from the true path] with their slogans of 'special socialism' or some sort of 'democracy' which savors of

[24] *Bashkimi* ("Union"), October 9, 1956.

anything but a proletarian spirit."[25] Hoxha thus left little doubt that he considered the Titoist heresy to be at the root of the troubles that threatened to disrupt the solidarity of the world communist movement.

Three days later, in his Pula speech, Tito expressed his own views on events in Poland and Hungary and he singled out the Albanian leaders for special criticism, characterizing Hoxha as a "would-be Marxist who knows how to utter 'Marxism-Leninism' and not a word more."[26] Tito made it clear that he believed the events of October and November stemmed not only from the cult of personality, but also from

. . . the bureaucratic apparatus, the methods of leadership and the so-called one-man rule, and the ignoring of the role and aspirations of the working masses, different Enver Hoxhas, Shehus, and other leaders of certain Western and Eastern parties who are resisting democratization and the decisions of the Twentieth Congress . . . and who are today working to revive [Stalinism] and to continue its rule.[27]

Either shortly before or after Tito's Pula speech the Soviet Ambassador to Tiranë, L. I. Krylov, informed Hoxha and the Albanian Central Committee of the contents of a note Khrushchev had sent to Tito on November 9. In this communication the Soviet party chief indicated the CPSU had initiated a move to replace Rakosi with Kadar in the summer of 1956.[28]

[25] For a translation of the Hoxha article, see Paul E. Zinner, ed., *National Communism and Popular Revolt in Eastern Europe* (New York: Columbia University Press, 1956), pp. 509–16.

[26] A translation of these remarks taken from *Borba* ("Struggle") for November 16, 1956 appears in *ibid.*, pp. 516–41.

[27] *Ibid.*, p. 519.

[28] *Zëri i Popullit*, November 8, 1961; January 9, 1962.

Hoxha was apparently both angered and disturbed by this disclosure.

Nevertheless, the Albanian press published, on November 23, 1956, a stinging reply to the Pula speech. It rejected the view that the Hungarian revolt had been inspired by the excesses of the Stalinists, Rakosi and Gerö, and blamed "the pernicious Yugoslav revisionist doctrines" and the Western imperialists. The Yugoslavs were further charged with seeking to overthrow the Albanian regime. As proof of this accusation, the Albanians revealed that three "Titoist spies," including a Yugoslav national, had just been executed for plotting against the state.[29]

At this point, hoping to calm the Albanians somewhat, *Pravda* printed on November 25, 1956, a half-hearted defense of Hoxha. While praising the Albanian Party chief for his loyalty to the principles of Marxism-Leninism, the Kremlin also mildly rebuked him for not being more tactful in his utterances toward the Yugoslavs and Tito.

Hoxha did receive a measure of support from the Chinese when on December 29, 1956, *Jen-min Jih-pao* published the text of a 15,000 word statement pleading for bloc unity and setting forth guidelines by which it might be preserved. Although the general tone of this statement was conciliatory, the Chinese did take the Yugoslavs to task for blaming all of the ills of the Communist camp on the legacy of Stalinism.[30] The Chinese, like the Albanians, but for different reasons, thus felt

[29] *Ibid.*, November 23, 1956.

[30] For a partial translation of the Chinese statement see David Floyd, *Mao against Khrushchev: A Short History of the Sino-Soviet Conflict* (New York: Frederick A. Praeger, 1963), pp. 242–46.

that bloc solidarity could be destroyed if Tito's views were allowed to stand unchallenged.

The Albanians were encouraged by the attitude of the Chinese and of Bulgaria, Czechoslovakia, and East Germany in respect to Titoism and de-Stalinization.[31] On February 13, 1957, Hoxha pressed his attack both against Tito and against the anti-Stalinists of the Soviet Union and the satellites in a fiery speech before the Central Committee of the APL. It was by far the most violent reaction to the de-Stalinization campaign, the Hungarian uprising, and the Yugoslav heresy to be voiced in the communist world up to that point, and it closely paralleled the Chinese statement of December 29 that Stalin's achievements greatly outweighed his shortcomings and that the mistakes he had made stemmed from his desire to protect the victory of communism in the Soviet Union and the integrity of the communist camp.[32]

However, even as Hoxha was continuing his attacks upon the Yugoslavs and the anti-Stalinists, Khrushchev with the aid of Chou En-lai was working feverishly to restore bloc unity. In January, 1957, Chou had made a hurried trip to Poland and Hungary to line up the new regimes in these states behind the Kremlin. Khrushchev at the same time began to summon the state and party leaders of the various satellites to Moscow to obtain from them a new pledge of loyalty to the U.S.S.R. and the CPSU. Hoxha and Shehu were the last of this group to make the pilgrimage to Moscow. Khrushchev had probably planned it this way in

[31] For the Bulgarian, Czechoslovak, and East German views on Titoism and de-Stalinization, see Brzezinski, *Soviet Bloc*, pp. 274–76, 280.

[32] Radio Tiranë, February 17, 1957.

order to convince the militant Albanians that they no longer enjoyed any support, since the other party states had one by one submitted to the wishes of the Kremlin.

During their sojourn in Moscow in mid-April 1957, the Albanian leaders, who fully appreciated their predicament, realized that they too had no choice but to accede to the demands made upon them by the Soviet Party and government. The Albanian delegation apparently had no qualms about subscribing to the desires of the Kremlin on ideological questions. These were largely based on the Chinese statement of December 29, 1956.[33] Hoxha and Shehu, however, were much more reluctant to abandon their feud with Tito, but at the repeated urging of Krushchev they finally agreed to make an effort to improve relations with Yugoslavia.[34]

The Albanians were amply rewarded for their cooperation. The U.S.S.R. cancelled the remaining payments of the 105 million dollars due on the credits and food made available to Albania between 1949 and 1957, and Moscow also agreed to furnish Tiranë with approximately 7.75 million dollars worth of foodstuffs during 1958 and step up her technical assistance program in Albania.[35]

When Hoxha and Shehu returned to Albania, a bitter debate within the Party over Yugoslav policy

[33] Brzezinski, *Soviet Bloc*, p. 281, has summarized the ideological principles to which the European satellites subscribed in their bilateral agreements with the Soviet Union in early 1957 as follows: "(1) Soviet primacy in proletarian internationalism (2) the struggle against imperialism internally and externally (3) the ubiquity of the concept of the dictatorship of the proletariat."

[34] *Zëri i Popullit*, April 15, 1957.

[35] *Pravda*, April 17, 1957.

resulted in the flight of the anti-Hoxha General Pana-
jot Plaku to Belgrade.[36] Hoxha and Shehu at this point
decided to tone down their anti-Yugoslav campaign in
order not to antagonize the U.S.S.R., whose economic
aid was essential for the success of the Second Five-Year
Plan.

In May, 1957, a Soviet delegation arrived in Tiranë
to advise the Albanians in the preparation of their
Fifteen-Year Prospective Plan (1961–1975) for economic development and to help coordinate this plan
with those of the other COMECON members. In August, Albania signed trade agreements with Hungary
and Czechoslovakia, whereby Albania would receive
industrial equipment and manufactured goods in return for mineral and agricultural products.[37]

By mid-autumn of 1957, economic conditions in Albania had improved to the point where the government was able to abolish food rationing, reduce food
prices, raise wages for most workers, and promise the
peasants higher prices for compulsory deliveries of
grain and meat.[38] The Albanian economy received another shot in the arm in November when the Soviet
Union granted Albania a new long-term credit of 40
million dollars.[39]

While domestic conditions in Albania improved,
relations with Yugoslavia remained tense. Although
the Albanians do not seem to have been eager to end
their ideological quarrel with the Yugoslavs, they do
seem to have made the effort to maintain correct, if

[36] Radio Moscow, July 25, 1964.
[37] For a summary of these developments, see Stephen D.
Kertesz, ed., *East Central Europe and the World* (Notre Dame,
Indiana: University of Notre Dame Press, 1962), pp. 210–12.
[38] Radio Tiranë, October 30, 1957.
[39] Radio Tiranë, November 24 and 26, 1957.

cool, political relations with Yugoslavia until October when both Tiranë and Belgrade resumed their polemics. In most other matters, however, the Albanians appear to have, at least publicly, followed the line set down by Moscow. One notable exception was the insistence of the Albanians, even after the successful testing of the Soviet intercontinental ballistic missile in August and the launching of Sputniks I and II in September and October, that the danger of imperialist aggression was becoming more acute.[40]

During 1957, as a consequence of the economic agreements concluded with the Soviet Union and the other Party states, bloc aid began to flow into Albania at an unprecedented rate. Albanian imports for the year totaled 2665.7 million leks ($53,314,000). Of this amount, the Soviet Union accounted for 48.5 per cent, with Czechoslovakia and China ranking second and third respectively.[41] As a result, the Second Five-Year Plan was revised upward, with a 55 per cent increase in the investment budget and the projected rise in industrial output set at 124 per cent instead of 92 per cent. It was also estimated that agricultural production by 1960 would be 76 per cent greater than in 1955.[42] A further indication of the improvement of economic conditions in Albania was the announcement of additional price reductions in April, 1958.[43]

In early May, shortly after the Seventh Congress of the Yugoslav League of Communists, the Albanians renewed their attack on Belgrade with their customary lack of restraint.[44] Although Albania was the first mem-

[40] *Bashkimi*, November 3, 1957.
[41] For Albanian trade figures for 1957, see *ESE*, 1960, chap. vi, p. 13.
[42] *Zëri i Popullit,* January 30, 1958 and March 4, 1958.
[43] Radio Tiranë, April 18, 1958.
[44] *Zëri i Popullit*, May 4, 1958.

ber of the Communist Bloc to react critically to the program adopted by the Yugoslav Congress, by the end of the summer of 1958 virtually every communist party and government had joined in condemning the new "revisionist theses" of Tito.

Hoxha now apparently thought that the time had come for him to press his quarrel with the Yugoslavs. In early June he went to Sofia to represent Albania at the Bulgarian Party Congress. With the exception of Khrushchev, Hoxha was the only other Party Secretary in attendance. He joined the other delegates in criticizing the "revisionist," "anti-Marxist," and "divisive" policies of the Yugoslavs.[45] Following the announcement of the execution of Imre Nagy on June 17, the Albanian press adopted the general bloc view that the deposed Hungarian leader had conspired with Tito to disrupt the unity of the communist camp.[46]

In the early summer of 1958, Hoxha attempted to create an anti-Tito coalition within the communist camp, and for this end he tried to strengthen his ties with two of the most outspoken critics of Yugoslav revisionism in Eastern Europe, Czechoslovakia and Bulgaria.

In August, following the arrest, detention, and subsequent execution of Hasan Spata, an Albanian subject who was passing through Yugoslavia on his way home, Albanian-Yugoslav relations took a turn for the worse. Tiranë branded Tito a "fascist" who had sold out to American imperialism and accused him of practicing genocide against the Albanian population of Kosovo. Belgrade revived its tales of the horrors of Albanian life under Hoxha and Shehu and castigated the Albanian leaders for their opposition to "every progressive

[45] Radio Sofia, June 4, 1958.
[46] *Zëri i Popullit*, June 21, 1958.

129

movement and trend in the socialist world." As 1958 drew to a close, a diplomatic break between the two states seemed inevitable.[47]

Although the Albanians were pleased by the new Soviet line toward Tito, they do not appear to have been completely satisfied. Hoxha and Shehu evidently would not rest easy until Yugoslavia had been finally and irrevocably read out of the communist movement and diplomatically isolated from the communist camp.

Second only to the Albanians in hostility toward the "revisionist" Yugoslavs were the Chinese, whose stand on this question strengthened their bonds with Albania despite the fact that internal difficulties forced China to cut drastically her exports to Albania. In addition, the Albanians endorsed the agricultural communes in China. It is interesting to note that they tended to agree with the Chinese on questions of global strategy as well, and that they both favored a militant, aggressive, communist foreign policy. This was especially true after 1957 when both Tiranë and Peking held that the preponderance of military power now lay in the communist camp.[48]

By the end of 1958, Hoxha was concerned not only by Khrushchev's unwillingness to make a final break with Tito but also by a new economic development which threatened to complicate his relations with Moscow. He was alarmed to learn that as COMECON had begun to draw up its long range plan for the integration of the bloc economies, it had relegated to Albania the task of supplying the member states with agricul-

[47] For these developments, see, *inter alia, Zëri i Popullit,* August 9, 10; October 20, November 7, 1958; *Borba,* September 26, 1958.

[48] For the developing Sino-Albanian entente, see, *inter alia, Zëri i Popullit,* October 20, November 13, 1958; *Bashkimi,* October 2, November 21, 1958.

tural and mineral raw materials. Hoxha was especially chagrined to find out that the discovery of new oil reserves in the U.S.S.R. and the subsequent decision to construct a pipeline from the Soviet Union into Eastern Europe would deprive Albania of the major market for her oil. The final blow came when the Soviet planners advised him to devote a greater share of Albanian investment funds to the agricultural sector of the economy, a recommendation which would undermine Hoxha's program of rapid industrialization.[49]

In mid-December, 1958, Hoxha and Shehu conferred with Soviet officials in Moscow about the future of the Albanian economy and were placated by a promise of additional Soviet economic assistance. Nevertheless, their apprehensions regarding Soviet policy toward Albania had not been laid to rest. In January, 1959, the Albanian leaders journeyed to East Germany and Czechoslovakia, two of the staunchest foes of Titoism, presumably to seek support for an anti-Tito faction within the communist camp. Neither the East Germans nor the Czechoslovaks responded favorably to this overture, and went no further than to issue perfunctory statements condemning "modern revisionism."[50] Shortly after their visits to East Germany and Czechoslovakia, Hoxha and Shehu returned to Moscow where they represented Albania at the Twenty-First Congress of the CPSU. For the most part, during 1959, the Albanian Party outwardly supported the policy pronouncements made by Khrushchev on this occasion.[51]

The most important area of Soviet-Albanian dis-

[49] Daniel Tretiak, "Khrushchev and Albania," *Problems of Communism*, XI, No. 7 (Jan.–Feb., 1962), p. 58.

[50] *Zëri i Popullit*, January 8, 1959; Radio Tiranë, January 12, 1959.

[51] See, for example, Enver Hoxha, *Fjalimi i mbajtur në*

agreement was the Yugoslav policy of the Kremlin. The Yugoslav-Albanian controversy continued unabated during the early months of 1959, although the two states had in early February signed a commercial accord. In mid-March the Yugoslavs withdrew their minister from Tiranë after announcing that they had jailed five Albanian spies. Not to be outdone, the Albanians disclosed in May that sixteen Yugoslav spies had been convicted by a court in Shkodër.[52] Albanian-Greek relations also became tense in the spring of 1959 following a clash between Greek and Albanian border patrols on March 30.[53]

At this point Khrushchev became disturbed by the ties between China and Albania. He decided to visit Tiranë in order to bring to an end Yugoslav-Albanian hostilities and to preserve Tiranë's loyalty to Moscow. Prior to his departure for Albania, the Soviet government set in motion the machinery for implementation of the economic aid promises given to Hoxha the previous December.[54] The Soviet Union was making every conciliatory effort to keep the Albanians from drifting closer to the Chinese and to coax them into muffling their criticism of Yugoslavia, whose support Khrushchev needed if his policy of establishing a missile-free, atom-free zone in the Balkans was to have any chance of success.

During his stay in Albania (May 25–June 4), Khrushchev lauded his hosts for their efforts to build

mbledhjen solemne me rastin e 15 vjetorit të çlirimit t'atdheut ("Speech Delivered at the Solemn Meeting on the Occasion of the 15th Anniversary of the Liberation of the Fatherland") (Tiranë: N. Sh. Botimeve "Naim Frashëri," 1959), pp. 20, 39–51.

[52] New York Times, March 15, 1959; Radio Belgrade, February 20, March 5, 7, 1959; Radio Tiranë, May 11, 1959.

[53] Zëri i Popullit, April 1, 1959.

[54] Tretiak, "Khrushchev and Albania," p. 59.

socialism along "correct Marxist-Leninist lines," issued a new call for the creation of a "peace zone" in the Balkans, and warned that if his appeal fell on deaf ears, it might be necessary to build rocket bases in Albania and Bulgaria to counter the threat of NATO installations in Greece, Italy, and Turkey. Hoxha, in addition to expressing his approval of Khrushchev's proposals, also promised that the Albanian Party and government would attempt to improve relations with Yugoslavia.[55] It was probably while he was in Albania that the Soviet dictator gave his approval to a 75 million dollar credit to Tiranë to help underwrite the Third Five-Year Plan in accordance with the promise he had made previously in December 1958.[56] Although Khrushchev made it clear that he felt Albania could make her greatest economic contribution to the bloc by further developing her agricultural potential, he apparently was willing to grant the Albanians a limited amount of economic freedom to gain their good will.[57]

Nevertheless, the Albanians continued to pursue a fairly independent course in their foreign and domestic policies. Although Tiranë endorsed the Soviet and Rumanian campaign to create a "peace zone" in

[55] *Zëri i Popullit*, May 31, 1959.

[56] The details of the Soviet credit were announced in July. Stanislaw Skrzypek, "Soviet Aid: A Balance Sheet," *East Europe*, XI, No. 8 (August 1962), p. 6.

[57] *Pravda*, June 7, 1959. Upon his return to the U.S.S.R., Khrushchev for the first time publicly hinted at the existence of difficulties between Moscow and Tiranë when he observed: "The more frequently statesmen, Party, and government figures meet with one another, the more candid their conversations, the more easily is mutual understanding achieved on specific issues, the more quickly are disagreements and rough spots eliminated. . . . In this respect, our trip to Albania was exceedingly beneficial." *Ibid.*

the Balkans, it had resumed open hostilities with Belgrade by the end of the summer and thus killed what little hope there had been that Yugoslavia would support this movement.[58] The Albanian policy of selective defiance of the Kremlin was also illustrated by the differing reactions of Tiranë on such issues as Khrushchev's 1959 visit to the United States and the Sino-Indian border clashes of that same year. In the first instance, the Albanians, following the lead of Moscow, hailed the Khrushchev journey to the United States as a constructive step in the direction of lowering world tensions.[59] On the other hand, Tiranë unlike Moscow was openly sympathetic to Peking during the Sino-Indian frontier crisis.[60] As 1959 drew to a close, the Chinese and Albanians found themselves in agreement, in opposition to the Kremlin, on such questions as Yugoslav revisionism, global strategy, and de-Stalinization.

By the beginning of 1960, the foundations of the Peking-Tiranë axis had been laid. While they made little secret of their sympathies for the Chinese stand on various ideological and political questions, Hoxha and Shehu nevertheless continued to pay lip service to the policy pronouncements from Moscow. They were still dependent on the Soviet Union for economic support and they had no desire to jeopardize the economy of the nation and perhaps even their own positions by precipitating a break with the Kremlin. They were probably reluctant to take any action which might tend to antagonize the Soviet Union until they were certain what the Chinese would do.

[58] Enver Hoxha, *Fjalimi i mbajtur ... me rastin e 15 vjetorit të çlirimit t'atdheut,* pp. 47–48.

[59] *Zëri i Popullit,* September 15, 1959.

[60] *Ibid.,* November 14, 1959.

5: THE SCHISM AND THE SINO-ALBANIAN ALLIANCE, 1960–64

The outbreak of Sino-Soviet polemics in April, 1960, probably marks the point at which the Albanian leaders began seriously to reappraise their relationship with the Soviet Union. Hoxha and Shehu appear to have decided in late May or early June to cast their lot with China. The first real evidence of Tiranë's drift into the Chinese camp appeared in June, when the Albanian delegation to the meeting of the General Council of the World Federation of Trade Unions (WFTU) in Peking joined with the Chinese in opposing the Soviets on several major questions. The views of the Albanian leadership were also indicated when pro-Moscow passages were deleted from the press reports of a speech delivered at a Sino-Albanian banquet by Liri Belishova.[1]

Khrushchev lost no time in reacting to the Albanian gestures of defiance. In early June he granted an interview to the influential Greek left-wing politician, Sophocles Venizelos. Although Khrushchev apparently did little more than promise Venizelos that he would explore with Hoxha the possibility of obtaining cultural autonomy for the Greek minority in southern Albania, the very fact that the Soviet leader had re-

[1] Griffith, *Albania*, pp. 37–39.

ceived Venizelos was cause for alarm in Tiranë, given the state of Greek-Albanian relations. It was probably the anxiety generated by this incident along with the increased Soviet activity within the ranks of the Albanian Party and armed forces that prompted Hoxha and Shehu to absent themselves from the Third Congress of the Rumanian Communist Party (June 20–25) in Bucharest.[2]

As is now known, Khrushchev attempted to transform the Bucharest Conference into a communist summit meeting for the purpose of securing the condemnation of the Chinese.[3] The chief Albanian delegate, Hysni Kapo, was the only representative of a European party state to refrain from criticizing Peking, to attack Yugoslav revisionism, and to refuse to alter his stand on the Chinese and Yugoslav issues despite the Soviet pressure.[4] Khrushchev's hopes of bringing the Albanians to heel by means of peaceful persuasion were certainly shattered by the time the Bucharest Conference had come to an end.

It was at this point that Moscow decided to initiate a

[2] In his speech of November 16, 1960 at the Moscow Conference of the 81 communist parties, Hoxha charged that the Soviet ambassador in Tiranë and his staff had "sown trouble" in the Albanian Party and had "gone so far as to precipitate a revolution in the army." For a summary of Hoxha's remarks at the Conference see Floyd, *Mao against Khrushchev*, pp. 289–91. The Albanian government appears to have launched its campaign against the anti-Hoxha elements in the Party and the Army in early July. *Le Procès contre le complot organisé pour liquider la République Populaire d'Albanie*, pp. 27–28.

[3] For brief accounts of the Bucharest Conference see Griffith, *Albania*, pp. 41–45; Donald S. Zagoria, *The Sino-Soviet Conflict, 1956–1961* (Princeton: Princeton University Press, 1962), pp. 325–27; and Edward Crankshaw, *The New Cold War: Moscow v. Pekin* (Baltimore: Penguin Books, 1963), pp. 97–110.

[4] For Kapo's address at the Conference see *Zëri i Popullit*, June 23, 1960; March 25, 1962.

new hard-line policy toward the recalcitrant Albanians. Since the Hoxha-Shehu ruling clique would not voluntarily retreat from its anti-Soviet stand, it would have to be forced to do so or be overthrown. Accordingly, the Soviets appear to have made a determined effort during the summer of 1960 to topple the Albanian leadership.

Moscow's campaign against Hoxha and Shehu was conducted on two levels, overt and covert. Publicly, the U.S.S.R. sought to capitalize on a drought-caused food shortage in Albania by delaying and drastically reducing grain shipments promised to the Albanians. The Soviet Embassy in Tiranë openly encouraged the pro-Soviet faction in the Albanian Party of Labor, led by Politburo member Liri Belishova and the veteran communist Koço Tashko, to work against the pro-Chinese orientation of the APL.[5] The Soviets also allegedly threatened to expel Albania from the Warsaw Pact with the implication that such an action would leave Albania at the mercy of her neighbors.

The Soviets also appear to have been involved in the preparation of an armed uprising by disaffected elements within Albania. This secret plot against the Hoxha regime, which was scheduled to break out in

[5] On September 8, 1960, Belishova was expelled from the Central Committee for "grave errors in respect to the party line" while Tashko was expelled from the Party and removed from his position as Chairman of the Central Auditing Committee for "hostile activity toward the party." *Zëri i Popullit*, September 9, 1960. Hamm, *Albania—China's Beachhead*, pp. 13–14, notes that Belishova and Tashko had made no secret of their pro-Soviet sentiments during the summer of 1960. A few weeks prior to her arrest, however, Belishova had embraced the pro-Chinese position of the Party leadership. This move, together with her distinguished war record and the fact that she had no real power base within the Party, probably accounts for the relatively light punishment she received from the APL.

the early autumn "on the eve of the Fourth Congress of the Albanian Party of Labor," was uncovered during the month of July by the Albanian security police. The leaders of this conspiracy were rounded up and in May, 1961, ten of them were tried publicly and convicted of various crimes against the state.[6]

Hoxha and Shehu were able to withstand the serious challenge to their leadership in the summer of 1960 because of the tight control they exercised over the party machinery. The Party in turn was able to maintain its firm grip on the security police and the armed forces, the mainstays of the Hoxha-Shehu regime. Furthermore, the Albanian leaders received both moral and material support from their Chinese allies. Peking's wheat shipments to Albania during the last half of 1960, for example, made it possible for Tiranë to continue to defy the dictates of Moscow.

By mid-August, when Khrushchev probably realized that his efforts to unseat the Albanian leaders had failed, he shifted his tactics. On August 13, 1960 the Central Committee of the CPSU sent a message to its Albanian counterpart, calling for bilateral talks between representatives of both parties in order to "extinguish the spark of misunderstanding before it becomes a fire." Two weeks later, the Albanians rejected the Soviet overture, which they realized was aimed at discrediting the position of the Chinese in the world communist movement and breaking the Sino-Albanian

[6] For the official Albanian version of this episode see *Le procès contre le complot organisé pour liquider la République d'Albanie*, pp. 3–445. The Fourth Congress of the APL was scheduled to meet in November. It was pushed back to December (*Zëri i Popullit*, October 9, 1960) and subsequently to February, 1961 (*ibid.*, December 21, 1960).

alliance.[7] Tiranë also took a strong pro-Chinese stand at the North Vietnamese Party Congress in early September.[8]

Khrushchev meanwhile openly snubbed Prime Minister Shehu, while maintaining most cordial relations with President Tito at the opening sessions of the United Nations General Assembly in late September. The Albanians responded by opposing in debate before the U.N. Political Committee a Soviet-backed Bulgarian proposal for total disarmament (except for police and frontier guards) in the Balkans.[9] Thus the Soviet-Albanian dispute was gradually becoming public.

It was against this background that the Moscow Conference of the eighty-one world communist parties convened on November 10, 1960. The Albanians were represented by Enver Hoxha, Mehmet Shehu, Hysni Kapo, and Ramiz Alija. Undoubtedly, the makeup of the Albanian delegation was designed to underscore the importance which Tiranë attached to this gathering, as well as to dramatize the unity of the Albanian leadership and the fact that it had crushed its opposition at home.

Khrushchev sought to take advantage of the presence of the Albanian leaders in Moscow by inviting them to meet with him on November 9, to discuss the differences between the two countries. On the eve of the Soviet-Albanian talks, however, Khrushchev, without warning, circulated among the communists assembled in Moscow a document condemning the Albanians for

[7] For an account of this Soviet-Albanian exchange see *ibid.*, March 25, 1962.

[8] *Ibid.*, September 8, 1960.

[9] *Ibid.*, October 13, 1960.

their "anti-Soviet policies and activities." The Albanians canceled the scheduled talks, but after two days of negotiation agreed to a second conference on November 12. Nothing constructive came out of this Soviet-Albanian encounter, since neither side was in a mood to compromise.[10]

The stage was now set for the public confrontation between the Albanians and the Russians before the assembled representatives of eighty-one world communist parties.[11] Enver Hoxha, the spokesman for the Albanian delegation, addressed the conference on November 16, two days after the Chinese.[12] He echoed the Chinese line on the major ideological, organizational, and political issues that divided Moscow and Peking. Discussing the crisis in Soviet-Albanian relations, he accused the U.S.S.R. of failing to consult Albania in matters concerning the Soviet and bloc policy toward Yugoslavia, encouraging Greek irredentist aspirations in southern Albania, fomenting "revolution" in the Albanian party and army, attempting to disrupt Sino-Albanian relations, applying economic pressure on Tiranë in an effort to force it to do Moscow's bidding, and threatening to expel Albania from the Warsaw Pact as well as from the communist camp itself. Hoxha left no doubt that he held Khrushchev responsible for the differences which had arisen between his country and the Soviet Union.

[10] For a brief summary of the November 1960 Soviet-Albanian negotiations from the Albanian point of view see *ibid.*, March 25, 1962.

[11] For useful general accounts of the November 1960 Moscow Conference see Crankshaw, *New Cold War*, pp. 116–35; Floyd, *Mao against Khrushchev*, pp. 110–29; Griffith, *Albania*, pp. 51–59; Zagoria, *Sino-Soviet Conflict*, pp. 343–69.

[12] For a summary of Hoxha's remarks see Floyd, *Mao against Khrushchev*, pp. 289–91.

Hoxha's speech acted as a release for the anger which had been building up in the ranks of the pro-Soviet delegations since the Chinese delegate had addressed the conference. Reluctant to criticize Peking directly, they could now indirectly strike back at the Chinese with impunity through the Albanians. For the next thirteen months Albania would enjoy an unaccustomed prominence in the communist world while it served as the proxy through which the U.S.S.R. and its allies carried on their struggle against China.

Hoxha and Shehu departed from Moscow on November 25, 1960, about a week before the conference ended, to celebrate at home the Albanian national holidays on November 28–29. The members of the Albanian delegation who stayed in Moscow until the end of the conference joined with the Chinese and the other parties in endorsing the vague and loosely worded Moscow Statement, which was in effect a thinly disguised attempt to compromise the conflicting Sino-Soviet viewpoints.[13] On December 20, the Central Committee of the APL unanimously approved the Moscow Statement. As might be expected, the Albanians stressed the sections of this document condemning U.S. imperialism and Yugoslav revisionism, while playing down those denouncing nationalism, dogmatism, and sectarianism.[14]

While the Moscow Conference was in session, an Albanian economic delegation under the leadership of Minister of Industry Xhafer Spahiu was engaged in negotiations with Soviet officials concerning the imple-

[13] For the official communiqué of the Moscow Conference see *Pravda*, December 1, 1960. The text of the Moscow Statement appeared in *Pravda* on December 6, 1960.

[14] For the Albanian Central Committee resolution see *Zëri i Popullit*, December 21, 1960.

mentation of promised Soviet aid for the period of the Albanian Third Five-Year Plan (1961–1965). After some two months of haggling, the Albanians were informed on December 20, 1960 that the Soviets would deal further only with Hoxha and Shehu concerning the economic relations between the two countries. On January 14, 1961, the Central Committee of the APL rejected Moscow's demands, which it regarded as an attempt to impose the will of the CPSU upon the Albanian leadership.[15]

By early January, 1961, Tiranë had recognized the futility of any further negotiations with Moscow and turned to Peking. On January 7, an Albanian economic mission departed from Tiranë for Peking. On February 2, the Chinese and Albanians concluded an agreement whereby China pledged to underwrite the construction and equipment of approximately twenty-five industrial enterprises during the period of the Third Five-Year Plan.[16]

Meanwhile, the newly appointed Soviet ambassador Joseph Shikin arrived in Tiranë apparently with instructions to make one final effort to bring the Albanians into line, but was received coldly.[17] At the same time, the Soviet technical advisers to the Albanian oil industry were recalled to Moscow upon the expiration of the Soviet-Albanian oil agreement of 1957, to warn the Albanians of the potential consequences of con-

[15] *Ibid.*, March 25, 1962.

[16] *Kongresi IV i Partisë së Punës së Shqipërisë* ("The Fourth Congress of the Albanian Party of Labor") (Tiranë: N. Sh. Botimeve "Naim Frashëri," 1961), p. 242. (Hereafter cited as *Kongresi IV i P. P. Sh.*) The details of the February 2 agreement were not revealed until April. N.C.N.A. (Peking), April 25, 1961.

[17] *Zëri i Popullit*, January 20, 1961.

tinued defiance of Russia.[18] The Albanians, however, remained firm in their determination to continue the struggle against "modern revisionism" irrespective of consequences and received encouragement from Peking in their struggle against "imperialism" and those groups which sought to defile "the purity of Marxism-Leninism."[19]

The foundations of the Sino-Albanian alliance had thus been firmly laid when the twice-postponed Fourth Congress of the APL began its week-long deliberations on February 13, 1961. In addition to the 803 delegates representing the 53,659 members and candidates of the Albanian Party, there were also in attendance representatives of 24 other communist parties.[20] With the exception of Yugoslavia, all of the party states sent delegations to Tiranë.[21] The proceedings of the Fourth Congress of the APL left no doubt that a serious split existed between Moscow and Tiranë and that there was little support for the Sino-Albanian position among the European communist parties.

In his opening address to the Congress, Hoxha restated his views concerning peaceful coexistence and criticized "those communists" who sought to preserve peace "by making concessions and flattering the imperialists" and those "revisionist" theoreticians who stressed the achievement of socialism by peaceful means and advocated economic decentralization. Obviously disturbed by the characterization of Albania as

[18] *Ibid.*, December 19, 1961. The Russians, however, maintained (Radio Moscow, December 29, 1961) that the Albanians "began to take concrete steps" to get rid of the Soviet experts during January, 1961.

[19] *Zëri i Popullit*, February 11, 1961.

[20] *Kongresi IV i P. P. Sh.*, p. 280.

[21] *Ibid.*, pp. 6–8. An additional fifteen parties sent messages of greeting to the APL. *Ibid.*, p. 371.

a Stalinist bureaucratic state, he declared that while
the Albanians recognized the dangers of bureaucratism,
they could not and would not weaken "the organs of
the dictatorship of the proletariat" so long as their
homeland and the socialist camp was threatened by
"imperialism, revisionism, and internal enemies."[22] A
major portion of Hoxha's speech was given over to an
attack on Tito's revisionism and Belgrade's anti-Albanian activities.

Shehu's remarks to the Congress were similar to
Hoxha's in content, but decidedly more violent and
emotional in tone.[23] Most of the foreign delegates had
listened in stony silence as Hoxha and Shehu delivered their harangues. Of the delegations present in
Tiranë only the Chinese, North Korean, North Vietnamese, Indonesian, and Japanese had endorsed, with
varying degrees of enthusiasm, the Albanian view-
point. The European parties, on the other hand, were
solidly opposed to the Albanian position. Not one of
the European party spokesmen praised Hoxha and
Shehu, while they all made at least formal professions
of loyalty to Khrushchev, whose name had not even
been mentioned by the Albanian leaders.[24] The tensions which had existed beneath the surface during the
Congress flared up briefly when the Greek delegate was
refused permission to address that body. Several of the
European delegations then joined the Greek delegation in protesting the conduct of the Albanians in
this matter.[25]

[22] For the text of the Hoxha speech, see *ibid.*, pp. 13–167.

[23] For the text of Shehu's address, see *ibid.*, pp. 171–266.

[24] For a useful summary of the views of the foreign delegations to the Fourth Congress, see Griffith, *Albania*, pp. 71–76.
For the texts of the remarks of the spokesmen of the visiting
delegations, see *Zëri i Popullit*, February 15–19, 1961.

[25] Griffith, *Albania*, pp. 75–76. For the Albanian version of
this episode, see *Zëri i Popullit*, February 16, 1962.

Not since the Yugoslav crisis of 1948 had a communist party publicly challenged the primacy of Moscow as had the Albanians at the Fourth Congress of the APL. Albania, unlike Yugoslavia in 1948, did not stand alone. In 1961, the APL enjoyed the support or sympathy of the Chinese and several other Asian communist parties. Khrushchev had to be careful to avoid aggravating the differences which had cropped up in the communist camp.

The Soviets realized that Albania was most susceptible to economic pressure. At the Fourth Congress of the APL, Hoxha and Shehu had announced that the main objectives of the Second Five-Year Plan (1956–1960), largely underwritten by the U.S.S.R., had been fulfilled.[26] The Albanian leaders noted that industrial production had risen 118 per cent between 1956–1960. This figure, they indicated, substantially exceeded the 92 per cent growth foreseen by the Plan.[27] While conceding that the agricultural sector of the economy had failed to meet its goals owing to unfavorable weather, Hoxha and Shehu pointed with pride to the fact that by the summer of 1960 approximately 86.3 per cent of the cultivated land in the country was collectivized[28]

The Third Five-Year Plan (1961–1965) was almost

[26] For Hoxha's and Shehu's analyses of the Second Five-Year Plan, see *Kongresi IV i P.P.Sh.*, pp. 52–72, 178–99.

[27] They conveniently overlooked the fact that the revised goals of the Second Five-Year Plan in February, 1958, called for industrial production to rise by 124 per cent between 1956–1960. See above, p. 128.

[28] During the Second Five-Year Plan Albanian agricultural production increased at the average annual rate of 1.2 per cent and supposedly achieved 76.5 per cent of its assigned goal. Misja, *Krijimi dhe zhvillimi i industrisë*, p. 167. This claim appears ridiculous in light of the extremely low average annual growth rate for the plan period. The revised agricultural plan proclaimed in February 1958 had predicted that production in 1960 would be 76 per cent greater than in 1955. See above, p. 128.

as ambitious as its predecessor. Industrial production was scheduled to rise by 52 per cent, agricultural production by 72 per cent, and national income by 56 per cent. Of the 69.5 billion leks ($1,390,000,000) budgeted to underwrite the plan, 54.1 per cent was allocated for industry, 12.8 per cent for agriculture, 12.7 per cent for transportation and communication, 14.6 per cent for social-cultural projects including housing, and 5.8 per cent for other sectors of the economy.[29] The investment priorities of the Third Five-Year Plan show that Hoxha and Shehu had not abandoned their program of rapid industrialization. This was in keeping with the long-range objectives of the Albanian leadership to make their country as self-sustaining as possible and to build socialism in accordance with the Soviet model. At the same time, however, it was evident that the Albanians could not hope to realize their economic objectives without substantial foreign assistance.

The Soviet government was well aware of the fact that the Albanians were counting heavily upon the approximately $132 million in credits which had been pledged or promised by the European Party states and China for the period of the Third Five-Year Plan. Although the Soviets knew that China and Albania had signed an economic pact in February, they were probably ignorant of the exact provisions of this agreement. Furthermore, the Russians may have convinced themselves that China, owing to her own economic plight, would be unable to fulfill the commitments she had made to Albania. In any event, the U.S.S.R. began to increase her economic pressure on Albania after the conclusion of the Fourth Congress of the APL. By the end of March, according to the Albanians, the Soviet

[29] For details of the directives of the Third Five-Year Plan, se *Kongresi IV i P.P.Sh.*, pp. 72–119, 199–243, 327–65.

and Czechoslovak governments had informed Tiranë that they intended to terminate their aid programs in Albania.[30] On April 26, 1961, the day after the terms of the February Sino-Albanian economic accords had been made public, Tiranë was officially notified that all Soviet economic aid programs in Albania would be discontinued immediately, owing to the "unfriendly policy" of the Albanian leaders toward the U.S.S.R. and the other socialist countries.[31] The impact of this Soviet gesture was lessened by the Chinese announcement, on April 25, of the February Sino-Albanian economic agreement, according to which Peking agreed to make available to Tiranë $123 million in aid and credits (approximately 90 per cent of the amount promised by the U.S.S.R. and the Eastern European countries) for the years 1961–65.[32]

At this juncture Soviet-Albanian relations deteriorated at an ever-increasing tempo. Between May 15 and May 27, 1961, the alleged leaders of the 1960 "Greek-Yugoslav-United States plot" to overthrow the APL were publicly tried in a Tiranë movie theater.[33] The ten defendents, who included Moscow-trained Rear Admiral Teme Sejko and Tahir Demi, former Albanian representative to COMECON, were accused of participating in a "revisionist, imperialist plot" to destroy the independence and integrity of Albania. Hoxha, Shehu, the Albanian Party of Labor, the armed forces, and the security police were cast in the roles of saviors of the Albanian nation and defenders

[30] *Zëri i Popullit*, December 6, 1961.
[31] *Ibid.*, March 25, 1962; May 17, 1964.
[32] N.C.N.A. (Peking), April 25, 1961.
[33] For the transcript of this trial see *Le Procès contre le complot organisé pour liquider la République Populaire d'Albanie*, pp. 3–445.

of Marxist-Leninist purity. The defendents in this show trial all admitted their involvement in the conspiracy against the regime and five of them received the death penalty. While the Albanians did not implicate the Soviet Union in this episode, they did display their displeasure with the Soviets by making Yugoslavia, the state which Moscow had painstakingly sought to restore to full membership in the communist camp, the chief culprit in this affair. The Russians in turn expressed their anger at Tiranë by ignoring the trial in their press and apparently urging the Eastern European party states to do likewise.[34]

By the end of May, according to Albanian sources, the U.S.S.R. began to dismantle its naval bases at Vlorë and Sazan.[35] The Albanians protested this action and sought to prevent the removal of the twelve Soviet submarines and their tenders. After bitter negotiations and perhaps even a skirmish with the Albanians, the Soviets were given permission to evacuate Vlorë, but only after they had agreed to leave behind four submarines, two tugs, and a quantity of radar and military equipment. In retaliation the Russians allegedly seized several Albanian warships then undergoing repairs at the Sevastopol navy yard.

As Soviet-Albanian relations worsened, Albania's ties with the East European Party states also became strained. During the summer of 1961, the East Europeans reduced the size of their embassy staffs in Tiranë, recalled their remaining technicians from Albania, canceled tours to Albania, and rescinded the scholarships of Albanian students and government per-

[34] *Zëri i Popullit*, November 8, 1961.
[35] *Ibid.*, May 10, 1966; July 21, 1966. For additional details concerning this episode see Heiman, "Peking's Adriatic Stronghold," pp. 15–17.

sonnel studying in their respective countries. Tiranë responded by imposing additional restrictions on the East European diplomats stationed in Albania.[36] The Albanians now began to boycott the meetings of intra-bloc organizations with increasing regularity.[37]

The leaders of the Albanian Party did, however, make an effort to effect a truce of sorts with the U.S.S.R. On July 6, 1961, the Central Committee of the APL dispatched a note to its Soviet counterpart stating that the Albanians were prepared to begin bilateral talks if the U.S.S.R. would take the necessary steps to normalize its diplomatic and economic relations with Albania.[38] The Central Committee of the CPSU not only rejected the Albanian conditions for bilateral negotiations, but also heaped new abuse upon the leaders of the APL, by branding them as "agents of foreign intelligence services."[39] Khrushchev was in no mood to compromise with the Albanians, whose continued defiance threatened to undermine his position as primate of the communist world.

Albanian-Soviet discord continued through the fall and the stage had thus been set for the showdown between Moscow and Tiranë at the Twenty-Second Congress of the CPSU, to which the Albanians had not been invited.[40]

[36] Hamm, *Albania—China's Beachhead*, pp. 29–37.

[37] From July to September 1961 the Albanians absented themselves from eighteen of the twenty-one meetings of intra-bloc organizations held during this period. Griffith, *Albania*, p. 84.

[38] *Zëri i Popullit*, March 25, 1962; February 7, 1963.

[39] *Ibid.*, March 25, 1962.

[40] For useful summaries and analyses of the Twenty-Second Congress of the CPSU, see Griffith, Albania, pp. 89–99, 102–5; Zagoria, *Sino-Soviet Conflict*, pp. 370–83; Hamm, *Albania—China's Beachhead*, pp. 140–66; Floyd, *Mao against Khrushchev*, pp. 143–52; Peter S. H. Tang, *The Twenty-Second Congress of the Communist Party of the Soviet Union and Moscow-Tirana-*

In retrospect it appears probable that the Khrushchev assault on the Albanians at the Congress was part of the Soviet dictator's campaign to reassert his leadership over the international communist movement in the face of growing opposition from Peking and Tiranë. On October 17, in his opening address to the Congress, Khrushchev criticized the leadership of the APL for having deviated from the principles of the 1957 Moscow Declaration and the 1960 Moscow Statement.[41] These pronouncements, at least insofar as the Soviet leadership was concerned, had made the policies of de-Stalinization, peaceful coexistence, and reconciliation with Yugoslavia adopted at the Twentieth Congress of the CPSU binding upon the members of the communist system. While Khrushchev's indictment of Tiranë and, by implication, Peking was severe, it was delivered in the tone of a wise parent scolding an errant offspring. In keeping with the general tenor of his remarks, the Soviet dictator concluded with a plea to the Albanians "to renounce their mistaken views and to return to the path of unity with the whole international communist movement."

If there had ever been any hope of effecting a reconciliation between Moscow and Tiranë at the Twenty-Second Congress, it was shattered by the speech of

---

Peking Relations (Washington: Research Institute on the Sino-Soviet Bloc, 1962), pp. 37–56; Carl A. Linden, *Khrushchev and the Soviet Leadership 1957–1964* (Baltimore: The Johns Hopkins Press, 1966), pp. 117–33. For abridged translations of the major speeches delivered at the Congress see Alexander Dallin, ed., *Diversity in International Communism: A Documentary Record 1961–1963* (New York: Columbia University Press, 1963), pp. 1–84. For a more detailed English translation of the proceedings, see Charlotte Saikowski and Leo Gruliow, eds., *Current Soviet Policies* IV (New York: Columbia University Press, 1962).

[41] *Pravda,* October 18, 1961.

Chou En-lai to the Congress on October 19,[42] and the publication the following day of a Statement of the Central Committee of the APL.[43] In his address Chou not only failed to follow the lead of Khrushchev in condemning the Albanians, but he also went so far as to criticize the U.S.S.R. for making its quarrel with Albania public. The statement of the APL Central Committee on October 20 blasted the "anti-Marxist, anti-Albanian actions" of Khrushchev at the Twenty-Second Congress. These, in the opinion of Tiranë, served only "the enemies of communism and the People's Republic of Albania, i.e., the imperialists and Yugoslav revisionists." Furthermore, the Albanians threatened to make available to the world communist parties the documentary record of the Soviet-Albanian dispute.

The Russian reaction was predictable. Each of the ranking members of the Soviet party hierarchy who addressed the Congress renewed and expanded the attack against Albania originally launched by Khrushchev.[44] In an attempt to convince the Albanians (and indirectly the Chinese) that they enjoyed little support within the ranks of the communist movement, the foreign delegates attending the Congress were encouraged to join in the denunciation of the APL. Of the sixty-six delegations that actively participated in the deliberations of the Congress, forty-four supported with varying degrees of enthusiasm the Soviet position on the Albanian issue.[45]

[42] *Ibid.*, October 20, 1961.

[43] Radio Tiranë, October 20, 1961. The Statement was published the following day in *Zëri i Popullit.*

[44] See *Pravda, October* 23–27, 1961.

[45] For an analysis of the stand of the foreign delegations, see Griffith, *Albania*, pp. 102–105; and Dallin, *Diversity*, pp. 83–84. Out of a total of eighty communist parties that either sent dele-

The Soviet anti-Albanian campaign reached its climax on October 27, when Khrushchev delivered his concluding speech to the Congress in which he reviewed the charges against the APL that had been made by the previous speakers, added a few details to illustrate the degeneracy of the Albanian leaders, and concluded by calling upon the Albanian people to overthrow Hoxha and Shehu.[46] Khrushchev left no doubt that he held the Albanian leadership responsible for the difficulties which had arisen between Moscow and Tiranë and also indicated his displeasure with the role of the Chinese in the Soviet-Albanian dispute. He therefore sought to embarrass the Chinese by inviting them to use their influence to resolve the differences that had arisen between Albania and the U.S.S.R.

Khrushchev's anti-Albanian tirade of October 27 was both a confession of his failure to bring Hoxha and Shehu into line as well as an appeal to the membership of the communist camp to expel the APL from their ranks. There were serious reservations concerning the wisdom of a harsh action against the Albanians, both within the leadership of the CPSU and among many of the foreign delegations at the Congress. These doubts were reflected in that section of the Congress' resolution dealing with the Albanian question which condemned the Albanians for their "unfounded and slanderous attacks" on the CPSU and their "fractionalist activity," but also invited them to renounce their errors and resume their place in the communist camp.[47]

---

gations or messages of greeting to the Congress, thirty-four did not join in the criticism of the APL and its leadership.

[46] *Pravda,* October 29, 1961.

[47] *Ibid.,* November 1, 1961. The relatively mild tone of the Congress' resolution on the Albanian question apparently re-

The Albanians, however, were in no mood to compromise, let alone "renounce their errors." Even while the Twenty-Second Congress of the CPSU was still in session, Hoxha and Shehu worked feverishly to rally the Albanian people around the regime by again raising the specter of foreign intervention. On November 7, Enver Hoxha delivered the first detailed Albanian reply to the charges that had been leveled against the leadership of the APL by the Soviets and their allies at the Twenty-Second Congress.

Hoxha's speech sounded the keynote for the violent public anti-Soviet campaign which the Albanians inaugurated in 1961.[48] He said that he held "Khrushchev and his group" mainly responsible for the difficulties between Moscow and Tiranë and confirmed that Soviet-Albanian relations had first become strained in the mid-1950s, when Khrushchev sought to effect a rapprochement with Tito's Yugoslavia. The proclamation of the de-Stalinization and peaceful coexistence policies by the Twentieth Congress of the CPSU and Khrushchev's insistence that these new lines be adopted by the world communist parties further exacerbated Moscow-Tiranë relations. While acknowledging political and personal differences between the leadership of the U.S.S.R. and Albania, Hoxha nevertheless sought to create the impression that his quarrel with Moscow was mainly ideological in nature.

---

flected the desire of some members of the CPSU Presidium, such as Kozlov and Suslov, to avoid doing anything that would further aggravate Sino-Soviet relations. See Linden, *Khrushchev*, pp. 131–33.

[48] For the text of this speech, see *Zëri i Popullit,* November 8, 1961. A translation of the major portion of this interesting and important speech appears in Dallin, *Diversity*, pp. 88–132.

Specifically, he charged that by misjudging the nature and strength of the imperialist camp the Soviets had betrayed the national liberation struggles being waged in Asia, Africa, and Latin America; furthermore, by elevating the concepts of peaceful coexistence and the peaceful transition to socialism into a long-range strategy, the Soviets were guilty of pursuing a "fraudulent and anti-Marxist course," which could only lead to a betrayal of world revolution and the negation of the class struggle. By persisting in their de-Stalinization policy, the Russians were giving aid and comfort to the opponents of communism and threatening the unity of the socialist camp.

Hoxha also castigated the CPSU for abandoning the struggle against Yugoslav revisionism and for violating the 1948 and 1949 Cominform resolutions expeling Tito from the communist camp, as well as the 1957 Moscow Declaration and the 1960 Moscow Statement. Hoxha left no doubt that he considered Khrushchev's attitude toward the Yugoslav issue to be the most serious error committed by the Soviet leader.

In addition to cataloguing their ideological differences Hoxha listed some of the political issues that had driven the two nations apart. These included Soviet hesitancy to force a settlement of the German question, Khrushchev's encouragement of Greek irredentist aspirations in southern Albania, and Moscow's policy of granting aid to "national bourgeois" regimes in the underdeveloped countries at the expense of lesser developed party states such as Albania. Hoxha also rejected the Soviet charge that he and his colleagues brutally violated the principles of party democracy in their administration of the APL. The Albanian Party Secretary indicated that he was privy to the tactics

Khrushchev had employed in his rise to power and that he was prepared to reveal all should the need to do so arise.

Finally, Hoxha noted that the proceedings of the Twenty-Second Congress of the CPSU had demonstrated that Albania "was not without friends in the Soviet Union and the socialist camp." The Albanians thus served notice that they had no intention of backing down. Indeed, as they received during November and December strong and repeated public endorsements of their policies from the Chinese, the Albanians pressed their quarrel with the Russians.[49]

On November 11, the Central Committee of the APL dispatched a note to its Soviet counterpart urging that body "in which the APL has had and still has unshakable confidence" to repudiate "the brutal anti-Marxist actions of N. Khrushchev and his group" toward the APL and the Albanian state.[50] While the Russians were angered by this gesture, which the Albanians did not publicize until March 1962, they were infuriated when Albanian embassies in Moscow and the other East European capitals began to distribute pro-Albanian propaganda to both diplomatic personnel and party leaders in these countries.[51]

The Russians responded to these new Albanian "provocations" on two levels—the ideological and the diplomatic. Beginning in mid-November, the pro-Soviet communist parties at Moscow's behest began to publish statements condemning the leadership and

[49] For useful summaries of the Chinese stand on the Soviet-Albanian dispute, see Griffith, *Albania*, pp. 111–29 *passim*; Tang, *Twenty-Second Congress*, pp. 77–90.

[50] *Zëri i Popullit*, March 25, 1962.

[51] *Ibid.*, December 10, 1961; Griffith, *Albania*, pp. 113–15.

policies of the APL.[52] Many of these anti-Albanian declarations were reprinted in *Pravda*. Moscow's strategy was obvious. It hoped to convince the Albanians that they enjoyed almost no support within the world Communist movement. The Albanians, however, refused to be intimidated. For that reason, on December 2, *Pravda* printed a long article by Yuri Andropov, the CPSU's specialist on relations with the ruling communist parties, which stated that loyalty to the policies of the Soviet Union and the CPSU was a prerequisite for membership in the socialist commonwealth.[53] Published on the eve of the Soviet-Albanian diplomatic rupture, the Andropov article was in effect a unilateral Soviet statement excommunicating the APL from the communist camp. On December 3, the U.S.S.R. broke diplomatic relations with Albania—an act without precedent in the history of the communist system.

In retrospect, it appears that Khrushchev felt constrained to carry his ideological struggle with the Albanians into the political arena, in order to preserve a modicum of discipline within the Communist camp, for had the Albanians been allowed to defy Moscow with impunity, this display of Soviet weakness would have encouraged the Chinese and other disgruntled parties to continue their fractional activity. It is interesting to note that no other party state followed the Soviet lead in breaking diplomatic ties with Albania. The East European communist states were content merely to recall their ambassadors and conduct relations through their chargés d'affaires in Tiranë. It is

[52] For translations of these anti-Albanian statements, see Dallin, *Diversity*, pp. 297–604 *passim*. For a complete listing of anti-Albanian statements of the world communist parties reprinted in *Pravda*, see *ibid.*, pp. 141–45.

[53] For a partial translation, see *ibid.*, pp. 605–16.

probable that the U.S.S.R. played a major role in shaping the Albanian policy of the party states. The Russians may have feared that if the East European party states joined with the Soviet Union to isolate Albania diplomatically and economically, Tiranë might be forced to turn to the West for aid, especially if China could not fill the gap created by the withdrawal of Soviet economic and technical assistance. If Albania had followed the road of Yugoslavia in this respect, the Russians would have laid themselves open to the charge that their policies had split the communist camp and served the interests of the imperialists. Not only would the Soviets have suffered a blow to their prestige in the international arena, but also Khrushchev's position in the CPSU would have been undermined.

While the Soviet-Albanian split was an accomplished fact, Sino-Soviet relations appeared to be taking a turn for the better in early 1962. By mid-January, 1962, Peking was no longer routinely reprinting all Albanian anti-Soviet pronouncements or publicly applauding the APL's defense of Marxism-Leninism. The Russians responded to these gestures by resuming cultural exchanges with the Chinese, concluding a new trade agreement with the CPR, and returning their ambassador to Peking. This Sino-Soviet détente stemmed from a concerted effort initiated by the North Vietnamese Workers (Communist) Party and endorsed by the communist parties of New Zealand, Indonesia, Sweden, and Great Britain to bring the Russians and the Chinese to the conference table, where they would hopefully resolve their differences, which threatened to disrupt the unity of the communist camp.[54]

[54] For brief accounts of these developments see Griffith, *Al-*

On February 22, 1962, the Central Committee of the CPSU sought to take advantage of the opportunity created by the North Vietnamese effort when it dispatched a note to Peking calling on the Chinese to halt their polemics and to withdraw their support from the Albanians. In their reply of April 7, the Chinese did agree to curtail their anti-Soviet propaganda activities, but made it clear that they had no intention of abandoning the Albanians and insisted that the U.S.S.R. take the initiative in normalizing relations with Albania, both on the party and state levels. On May 31, the Russians rejected the conditions regarding the Albanian question that had been laid down by Peking. Moscow stressed that there could be no reconciliation with Tiranë until the Albanians had repudiated their anti-Soviet stand.[55] Khrushchev thus served notice that he would accept nothing less than the total surrender and humiliation of the Albanians as his price for restoring them to full-fledged membership in the communist camp.

It was against the background of this Sino-Soviet détente that the Albanians in mid-April ceased their direct anti-Soviet polemics, which had reached a fever pitch during the latter part of March. There is little

bania, pp. 143–44; Dallin, *Diversity*, pp. 650–52; Floyd, *Mao against Khrushchev*, pp. 156–57. For a more detailed analysis see William E. Griffith, *The Sino-Soviet Rift* (Cambridge: The M.I.T. Press, 1964), pp. 33–42.

[55] For the Sino-Soviet exchanges between February and May, 1962 see Griffith, *Sino-Soviet Rift*, pp. 36–37; *Lindja dhe zhvillimi i divergjencave midis udhëheqjes së PK të Bashkimit Sovjetik dhe PK të Kinës*, I ("The Birth and the Development of the Differences Between the Leadership of the C[ommunist] P[arty] of the Soviet Union and the C[ommunist] P[arty] of China") (Tiranë: N.Sh. Botimeve "Naim Frashëri," 1964), pp. 41–42.

doubt that the Albanians had suspended their polemics at the suggestion of the Chinese, but this gesture was in vain, since the Russians had no intention of negotiating seriously their differences with Tiranë. Just as the Albanians were bringing their anti-Soviet activities to a halt the U.S.S.R. began to court Yugoslavia and the Albanians were excluded from the June meetings of COMECON and the Political Consultative Committee of the Warsaw Pact. Obviously, Khrushchev was more interested in humbling the Albanian leaders than in finding some mutually acceptable face-saving formula to heal the Soviet-Albanian rift.

Thus, by mid-July, 1962, all hope of a Soviet-Albanian reconciliation was shattered and Tiranë resumed its anti-Russian, anti-revisionist propaganda campaign, with much effort devoted to denouncing the growing Soviet-Yugoslav rapprochement. In mid-September, on the eve of the visit to Yugoslavia of Leonid Brezhnev, at that time the Soviet head of state, the Albanians charged that the Russians and Yugoslavs were forging an alliance between the "revisionists" and the "imperialists" in order to "liquidate socialism."[56] Shortly after Brezhnev's departure from Yugoslavia, the Albanians unleashed what was up to that time their most violent personal attack on Khrushchev. They not only called for the overthrow of the Soviet dictator, but also urged the world communist parties to renounce their allegiance to Moscow and to rally behind Peking and Tiranë, the champions of Marxist-Leninist orthodoxy.[57]

By the end of October, Soviet-Albanian polemics became more violent as Tiranë lashed out against Mos-

[56] *Zëri i Popullit*, September 19, 20, 1962.
[57] *Ibid.*, October 13, 1962.

cow for its failure to back the Chinese during the October, 1962, Sino-Indian border conflict and for having bowed before U.S. pressure during the Cuban missile crisis of the same month. According to the Albanians, Khrushchev's stand in both the Cuban affair and the Sino-Indian border conflict provided incontrovertible proof that the "revisionist" Soviet leadership had betrayed the world communist movement and was actively working with the imperialists to destroy it.[58]

The extent to which Albania's hard-line anti-Soviet policies had isolated her from the remainder of the communist camp was graphically demonstrated during November and December, 1962, when the APL was not invited to send a delegation to the Congresses of the Bulgarian, Hungarian, Czechoslovakian, and Italian communist parties.[59] The APL was the only ruling communist party to be accorded such treatment. This gesture, especially on the part of the three ruling East European communist parties whose governments still maintained diplomatic and commercial relations with Tiranë, was probably designed to underscore Albania's outcast status in the world communist movement.

The Albanian leaders and their policies were condemned at each of the party congresses and only China, which was represented at all four of them, came to the defense of the Albanians. But by late 1962, the Chinese also found themselves on the defensive as the pro-Soviet parties became more outspoken in their criti-

[58] *Ibid.*, November 4, 8, 1962.

[59] For useful summaries of the developments at the European communist party congresses, see Griffith, *Sino-Soviet Rift*, pp. 67–84; Dallin, *Diversity*, pp. 660–67; Floyd, *Mao against Khrushchev*, pp. 161–63, 325–26.

cism of Peking. With the Sino-Soviet rift gradually becoming public, Albania's role as one of the major proxies through which Peking and Moscow had conducted their polemics was coming to an end.

During November and December of 1962, irritated by the repeated Albanian appeals to the world communists for the overthrow of Khrushchev and the repudiation of "modern revisionism," Moscow in retaliation escalated its anti-Albanian propaganda campaign. The Soviets now charged that the policies of the leaders of the APL had driven Albania into the anticommunist camp. Hoxha and Shehu were further warned that the Soviet people could not long "remain indifferent to the fate of the fraternal Albanian people whose socialist achievements [were] endangered by the adventurous policy of their leaders. . . ."[60] Khrushchev had again placed the Albanians on the alert by his implied threats against the leadership of the APL. The anxiety of the Albanians was further heightened by Tito's visit of December 4–20 to the U.S.S.R.

It was therefore not surprising that, on December 12, Khrushchev denounced in the Supreme Soviet the policies of the APL.[61] After defending his conduct in the Cuban crisis and the Sino-Indian border conflict, he castigated the Albanians as "the most open spokesmen [of] the present-day left-wing opportunists and sectarians" for refusing to see the error of their ways. Khrushchev also infuriated Tiranë by stating that, according to "the objective laws of Marxism-Leninism," Yugoslavia was "a socialist country." To emphasize further the growing Soviet-Yugoslav rapprochement,

[60] *Izvestia*, November 27, 1962.
[61] *Pravda*, December 13, 1962. For an English translation of the major portion of this speech, see Dallin, *Diversity*, pp. 670–95.

Tito addressed the Supreme Soviet on December 13.

By mid-December the Albanians sought to discredit Moscow's pro-Yugoslav policy in a series of rejoinders to the Khrushchev speech. On December 13, *Zëri i Popullit*, after analyzing the draft of the new Yugoslav constitution, observed that "far from being a socialist constitution it [was] a typical bourgeois constitution clothed in socialist garments." In one of its first comments on the treatment accorded Albania at the European party congresses, Tiranë charged that "the entire revisionist chorus of Khrushchev . . . and others had deliberately set out to discredit the APL which had foiled their plans [to effect an alliance between 'modern revisionism' and 'imperialism'] and unmasked their treachery."[62]

But despite Tiranë's pretentious claim to be the guardian of Marxist-Leninist orthodoxy, Albania, after the outbreak of direct polemics between Moscow and Peking in early 1963, began to play a subsidiary role in the Sino-Soviet dispute. Tiranë now began to follow more conspicuously the lead of Peking in the conduct of its anti-Soviet campaign. The Soviet Union at the same time seemed to be making a deliberate effort to downgrade the importance of Tiranë. On February 21, 1963, the Central Committee of the CPSU had dispatched to its Chinese counterpart a letter proposing bilateral talks between the two parties as a preliminary step to the convocation of an international conference of communist parties to resolve the differences that had split the ranks of world communism.[63]

The CPSU did not feel constrained to make any

[62] *Zëri i Popullit*, December 16, 1962.

[63] A translation of this Soviet letter, which was originally published in *Pravda* on March 14, 1963, appears in Dallin, *Diversity*, pp. 814–19.

overtures to the APL until the Chinese in their reply to the Soviets on March 9 again, as they had in 1962, urged Moscow to take the initiative in normalizing relations with Tiranë. It was therefore not until March 11, after they had received the Chinese reply, that the Soviets dispatched a note of "a few lines" and a copy of the February 21 letter of the CPSU to the APL. The Albanians were especially angered by the implication that they were mere dependencies of the Chinese Communist Party. Accordingly, in its reply to the Soviet note on March 13, the Central Committee of the APL stressed that Tiranë was not prepared to take part in any bilateral discussions with the Russians until "the CPSU Central Committee establishes all the conditions of total equality [between the parties]. . . ."[64]

On April 3, the Soviets publicized their efforts to regularize relations with Tiranë.[65] The implication was clear. Moscow had made a genuine effort to heal the breach with the Albanians. Since the APL had failed to respond positively, it must now bear the burden for the perpetuation of the Moscow-Tiranë rift, which the Chinese viewed as a major stumbling block to the resolution of the Sino-Soviet dispute and the restoration of unity to the communist camp.

The Albanians naturally refused to accept this interpretation. Tiranë made it evident that it doubted the sincerity of the Soviet overture, since the Russians had done nothing to change those policies—especially in respect to Yugoslavia—which had precipitated the

[64] For the Albanian version of these events, see *Zëri i Popullit*, April 18, 1963.

[65] See *Pravda*, April 3, 1963. The Soviets maintained that they had invited the APL in late February to participate in bilateral negotiations with representatives of the CPSU. According to the Russians, the Albanians did not acknowledge the letter or reply until much later (March 13).

Soviet-Albanian rift. The Albanian leaders were especially angered by Moscow's attempt to make the recognition of Yugoslavia as a full-fledged "socialist country" and the Yugoslav League of Communists as a "fraternal party" by the Chinese a *quid pro quo* for a similar concession in respect to Albania and the APL by the U.S.S.R.[66]

It would appear that the U.S.S.R. in its approach to the Albanian issue during the early part of 1963 was more interested in scoring propaganda points than in resolving the Soviet-Albanian break. The CPSU's assertion that the APL's unwillingness to negotiate on Moscow's terms would hinder direct Sino-Soviet discussions was found wanting when China and the Soviet Union agreed to initiate high-level party discussions in July in the Soviet capital. It is also worthy of note that the U.S.S.R. made no effort to halt the violent anti-Chinese propaganda campaign mounted by the Yugoslavs. Furthermore, the renewal of Sino-Soviet tensions in Central Asia during the spring and summer of 1963 killed what little hope there had existed for a reconciliation between Moscow and Peking. The Albanian issue at this point had receded to a position of secondary importance.[67]

The expected failure of the Sino-Soviet discussions held between July 5 and July 20, the conclusion of the U.S.–Soviet Limited Nuclear Test Ban Treaty on August 5, and the Khrushchev visit to Yugoslavia, between August 20 and September 3, all served to dramatize the seriousness of the Sino-Soviet dispute. Indeed, by the autumn of 1963, Khrushchev was promoting his

[66] *Zëri i Popullit*, April 18, 1963.
[67] For a general discussion and analysis of these developments see Griffith, *The Sino-Soviet Rift,* pp. 124–53, and Floyd, *Mao against Khrushchev,* pp. 181–90.

scheme for the convocation of an international conference of communist parties, ostensibly to heal the
Sino-Soviet rift, but actually to read the Chinese out
of the world communist movement. When Khrushchev's plans were thwarted, the Albanians, who were
more eager than the Chinese to provoke a showdown
with the Russians and to embarrass Khrushchev, appear to have been disappointed.[68]

As 1963 drew to a close, the Albanian leaders were
making a concerted effort to create the impression that
Tiranë and Peking enjoyed widespread support in the
communist camp. The Albanian press and radio began
to publicize extensively the activities of the pro-Peking
splinter factions which were being organized, especially
in Western Europe, at this time.[69]

As Albania's role in the Sino-Soviet dispute continued to decline in importance, the Albanian leaders
were apparently anxious to enhance their prestige and
raise the morale of their people. On December 24,
Tiranë announced that Prime Minister Chou En-lai,
Foreign Minister Ch'en Yi, and a delegation comprised
of lesser ranking party and state dignitaries would pay
a ten-day visit to Albania. Chou's trip to Albania,
which was made in conjunction with his tour of Africa,
was a complex, multi-dimensional diplomatic undertaking. It was, of course, primarily designed to calm
the fears of the Albanian people and raise the prestige
of the Albanian leaders by providing concrete evidence
of the close ties existing between Peking and Tiranë.
Second, by visiting Albania, Chou may have sought
to convince Khrushchev that China had no intention
of abandoning its Albanian ally and to demonstrate

[68] *Zëri i Popullit,* October 4, 1963.
[69] See, for example, *Zëri i Popullit,* November 12, 17, 21,
1963.

that Peking had established a beachhead in Eastern Europe. Third, the Chinese leaders probably wished to convince their own people, most of whom very likely had no real conception of the size or importance of Albania, that China enjoyed the support of European as well as Asian party states.

Chou and his entourage toured Albania for ten days (December 31, 1963–January 9, 1964), visiting every major city and virtually every significant industrial establishment in the country.[70] The high point of Chou's visit came on January 8, when at a mass rally in Tiranë, the Chinese Prime Minister praised the Albanian people for the struggle they had successfully waged against United States imperialism and Yugoslav revisionism to preserve the independence and integrity of the People's Republic of Albania. He congratulated the leadership of the APL and the Albanian people for having remained true to the principles of Marxism-Leninism in the face of pressures brought against them by the "modern revisionists."[71]

Following the departure of Chou, the Albanians, buoyed by the visit of the Chinese, gradually escalated their anti-Soviet polemics. By late February, Soviet-Albanian hostility reached a new peak as a consequence of the Albanian seizure of the abandoned buildings of the Soviet Embassy in Tiranë.[72] The publication on April 3 of the Suslov Report to the Feb-

[70] For the activities of the Chinese delegation, see *ibid.*, January 2–11, 1964. Radio Tiranë, December 31, 1963–January 9, 1964, also provided extensive coverage of the Chinese visit.

[71] Radio Tiranë, January 8, 1964.

[72] For the Soviet version of this episode, see *Izvestia*, February 24, 1964. For the Albanian version, see *Zëri i Popullit*, February 28, 1964.

ruary, 1964, meeting of the Central Committee of the CPSU further annoyed Tiranë.[73] In his report, which analyzed the factors that had produced the Sino-Soviet rift and recommended the convocation of an international conference of communist parties to resolve the difficulties plaguing the communist camp, Suslov had dismissed the Albanians as mere "tools" of the Chinese.

In replies to this Soviet attack, the Albanian press stressed that Moscow was trying to replace Marxism-Leninism with "Khrushchevism," and like earlier attempts to dethrone Marxism-Leninism this assault would also be thwarted.[74] On May 17, Tiranë printed a detailed response to the Suslov report.[75] After branding Khrushchev guilty of having provoked the Sino-Soviet dispute, the Albanians identified themselves with the Chinese position on those issues that had divided world communism, rejected the Soviet view that they were mere "tools" of the Chinese, and set forth the conditions under which they would be willing to attend a conference of world communist parties. Among other things, the Albanian leaders demanded that the new pro-Peking "Marxist-Leninist" parties be invited to join in the work of the congress while Yugoslavia be excluded; all outstanding differences of a specific nature between communist parties be resolved; and Khrushchev and his allies in Eastern Europe "publicly and honestly" admit the errors they

[73] *Pravda*, April 3, 1964.
[74] See, for example, *Zëri i Popullit*, April 22, May 1, 1964. On April 17, Radio Tiranë had announced that the city council of Tiranë had revoked the honorary citizenship it had bestowed on Khrushchev in 1959.
[75] *Zëri i Popullit*, May 17, 1964.

had committed in their relations with Albania. The Albanian stand was clear. Tiranë would not take part in an international conference of communist parties unless its participation was preceded by extensive preparatory work, bilateral negotiations, and a public confession by Khrushchev of his sins. The Albanian terms were obviously unacceptable to Moscow and the Soviet-Albanian discord continued throughout the summer.

6: THE PRESENT STAGE: SUMMARY AND CONCLUSIONS

On October 14, 1964, Khrushchev fell from power. Tiranë hailed this development as "a great victory for the Marxist-Leninist forces in their resolute struggle against the modern revisionists [and] a testimony to the well known policy of our party," but the Albanian press and radio were guarded in their comments concerning the new Soviet leadership. When it became evident that Brezhnev and Kosygin did not contemplate significant changes in Soviet policy, Tiranë gradually resumed its hostilities with Moscow.[1]

In early November, the Albanian leaders felt constrained to outline their conditions for a Soviet-Albanian reconciliation. Specifically, they demanded that the Soviets rehabilitate Stalin, engineer the overthrow of Tito, repudiate revisionism, and restore "Leninist norms" in the organization of the CPSU.[2]

When it became obvious that the new Soviet leaders had no intention of giving serious consideration to the Albanian proposals, Tiranë responded on November 13, by publishing an extensive critique of the political "Testament" of Palmiro Togliatti, the long-time secretary of the Communist Party of Italy. The Albanians

[1] Radio Tiranë, October 17, 20, 1964.
[2] *Zëri i Popullit*, November 7–8, 1964.

169

noted that they had withheld publication of this article, which was ready for the press when Khrushchev was ousted, in the hope that the new Soviet leaders would renounce the revisionist course they had pursued since 1956. Instead of abandoning revisionism, however, Khrushchev's successors had become partisans of Togliatti, whose views in the eyes of Tiranë were more radically revisionist than those of Tito.[3]

Thus within a month after the fall of Khrushchev, Tiranë had come to the conclusion that there was no possibility of reaching an accommodation with the Soviet Union. Accordingly, the Albanian anti-Soviet propaganda campaign again moved into high gear, and on November 28, Hoxha delivered a violent personal attack on Brezhnev, Kosygin, Mikoyan, and Suslov.[4]

Meanwhile the U.S.S.R. did little to conciliate the Albanians. Albania was the only party state not invited to participate in the forty-seventh anniversary celebration of the Bolshevik Revolution. The Soviet government did send perfunctory greetings to the Albanian people on the occasion of the twentieth anniversary of the liberation of Albania from the Axis occupation, but this was in marked contrast to the warm congratulatory message sent to Tito and the Yugoslav people the same day.[5] Albania's isolation was again underscored when only five ruling parties (China, North Korea, North Vietnam, Rumania, and Cuba) sent delegations to participate in the Albanian celebration.[6]

Perhaps in the hope of reversing Tiranë's drift from the main body of the communist camp, the Soviet

[3] *Ibid.*, November 13, 1964.
[4] Radio Tiranë, November 28, 1964.
[5] See *Pravda*, November 29, 1964, for both messages.
[6] Radio Tiranë, November 25–December 6, 1964.

Union invited Albania through Poland to participate in the January meeting of the Political Consultative Committee of the Warsaw Pact. On January 15, 1965, Tiranë responded to this overture. While making it clear that they still regarded themselves as members of Warsaw Pact, the Albanians rejected the invitation. They then set forth the conditions that had to be fulfilled before they would resume their rightful place in the organization. Tiranë insisted that the member states join in condemning the "illegal and hostile" Soviet actions against Albania, and that the U.S.S.R. compensate the Albanians for the economic and military aid they had lost as a consequence of the Soviet-Albanian break, for which Moscow was to admit its responsibility.[7] The Warsaw Pact signatories apparently never even bothered to answer the Albanian note.

China's continuing support of Albania was again demonstrated in late March when Chou En-lai, accompanied by a high-ranking delegation, made a brief visit to Albania while returning home from the funeral of Gheorghe Gheorghiu-Dej in Rumania. During his stay in Albania the Chinese Prime Minister emphasized a new theme which held that China and Albania were in the vanguard of the anti-imperialist movement. In an obvious appeal to the political leaders of the developing nations, Chou observed that "to carry on a true fight against the American imperialists is the main criterion for distinguishing the Marxist-Leninists from the modern revisionists."[8]

The Albanians undoubtedly took advantage of the presence of the Chinese Prime Minister to lay the groundwork for the Sino-Albanian economic talks scheduled for late April in Peking and designed to

[7] *Zëri i Popullit*, February 3, 1965.
[8] Radio Tiranë, March 29, 1965.

work out the details of the Chinese economic and technical assistance programs for the period of the Albanian Fourth Five-Year Plan (1966–70).

A fifteen-man Albanian delegation headed by First Deputy Prime Minister Spiro Koleka, one of Albania's leading economic planners, departed for China on April 23, and was engaged in negotiations with the Chinese from April 26 to June 8, when a Sino-Albanian credit agreement was concluded.[9] The length of the discussions, coupled with the fact that the terms of the Sino-Albanian credit agreement have never been officially revealed,[10] seems to indicate that the Chinese, owing primarily to their own economic difficulties, were unable to provide the Albanians with the quantity of aid they desired.

During the spring and summer of 1965, the Albanians and the Chinese began to develop the propaganda line that the "revisionist, opportunistic" foreign policy of the U.S.S.R. was betraying the national liberation struggle of the Vietnamese people.[11] Tito's visit to the U.S.S.R. in late June provided additional proof to the Albanians that Russia's new rulers were no improvement over Khrushchev.[12]

But by 1965, the leaders of the APL were perhaps even more concerned about the emergence of revisionist tendencies within Albania than with revisionist tendencies abroad. The internal stability of Albania was apparently threatened in several areas. There was

[9] *Ibid.*, April 23, 26, June 9, 1965.

[10] Estimates of the value of the Chinese credit for the period of the Fourth Five-Year Plan range from $60 million (*New York Times,* May 31, 1966) to $214 million (Prybyla, "Albania's Economic Vassalage," p. 10).

[11] See for example *Zëri i Popullit,* April 20, June 1, 27, 1965. N.C.N.A. (Peking), June 13, 1965.

[12] *Zëri i Popullit,* July 10, 1965.

a breakdown in discipline in some local party units, where most of the difficulty was caused by personal rivalries and by the desire of the local party elite to use their positions for personal advantage. In some areas, party meetings had degenerated into brawls and shouting matches.[13] A new wave of literary ferment was sweeping through the country. Some writers were beginning to break away from the strictures of socialist realism and to stress humanistic themes. So great was the threat in this area, that the October plenum of the Central Committee was devoted to this problem.[14] Owing in part to the failure of the Chinese to furnish the goods and services they had pledged at the beginning of the Third Five-Year Plan and to poor economic planning and administration, Albania was plagued with inflation during 1961–65 and there was much grumbling over low productivity and poor quality of workmanship. To remedy this situation the *lek*, the standard unit of currency, was revalued (10 old *leks* = 1 new *lek*) and discussions were initiated at the local units of production aimed at finding solutions to the problems troubling the economy.[15] The Albanian regime felt impelled to take drastic action to safeguard its position at the beginning of 1966.

Albania's domestic difficulties had not gone unnoticed within the communist camp. During the early part of 1966, amid rumors of an impending Sino-Albanian split, the U.S.S.R. and her allies made a concerted effort to wean Albania away from China.[16] On

[13] *Ibid.*, March 12, 1965.

[14] *Drita* (Tiranë), April 18, 1965; *Zëri i Popullit*, October 26. 29, 1965.

[15] *Ibid.*, May 21, July 7, November 8, 1965; Radio Tiranë, July 15, 1965.

[16] *New York Times.* February 12, 1966; *Christian Science Monitor*, February 21, 1966.

January 5, 1966, Albania was invited along with other signatories of the Warsaw Pact and the "socialist countries of Asia" to participate in a conference which was designed to find a formula whereby the communist nations might coordinate their aid to the Viet Cong and North Viet Nam. Tiranë refused to attend this meeting unless the Soviet Union and the Eastern European communist parties "publicly acknowledged the injustice" they had perpetrated against Albania.[17] In February, the Albanians also rejected a Soviet offer to resume commercial relations.[18]

In order to dispel the widespread rumors that a serious misunderstanding had cropped up between Tiranë and Peking, Mehmet Shehu was sent to China along with a group of high ranking Albanian Party and government functionaries. During their stay in China (April 28–May 12), Shehu and his party were accorded an unusually warm reception and granted a private audience with Mao Tse-tung.[19] If any serious disagreements had previously existed between Tiranë and Peking, they appeared to have been completely resolved.

The ouster of Yugoslav Vice-President Ranković in early July resulted in a new outbreak of Albanian-Yugoslav polemics and further minimized any possibility that Tiranë might gravitate from the Chinese orbit. Soviet-Albanian relations also remained tense during the autumn of 1966. On September 16, the Albanians announced with a great deal of fanfare that

[17] Radio Tiranë, February 12, 1966.
[18] Radio Moscow, June 30, 1967. Tiranë also rejected a Soviet invitation to send a delegation to the Twenty-Third Congress of the CPSU. Zëri i Popullit, March 22, 1966.
[19] For coverage of the Shehu trip see ibid., April 29–May 14, 1966.

they had completed, by their own efforts, the Palace of Culture in Tiranë, which had been initiated by the Russians and temporarily abandoned following the Soviet-Albanian break.[20] The Albanian-constructed Palace of Culture now became the national symbol of Tiranë's successful defiance of the Kremlin.

But Albania had paid a heavy price for her defiance of the U.S.S.R. Her economy was beset with difficulties during the period of the Third Five-Year Plan (1961–1965) and these economic problems appear to have been a major factor in triggering off the unrest that began to spread throughout Albania during 1965 and 1966.

The Albanian leaders were deeply concerned by the growing alienation of the masses from the regime. They also began to have serious misgivings about the dangers posed to the regime by the emergence of the large party and state bureaucracy which now stood as a barrier between the rulers and the people. In February, 1966, therefore, the leaders of the APL initiated what has come to be called the Albanian Cultural Revolution. Unlike its Chinese counterpart, the Albanian Cultural Revolution was not designed to mask an intra-party power struggle, but represented a unified effort by the leadership of the APL to reassert its authority over the regional and local party organizations, rally the people behind the regime, and reestablish the party's influence in all sectors of Albanian life.

The Albanian Cultural Revolution was inaugurated in February, 1966, with the announcement that a number of high ranking party and state functionaries had been assigned to work with local and regional party

[20] Radio Tiranë, September 16, 1966.

175

and state organs.[21] Next, the APL sought to reduce the swollen ranks of the bureaucracy by encouraging excess personnel to "volunteer" for productive work in factories and on farms.[22]

In early March, the APL issued an Open Letter to the People in which it promised to correct its failures and shortcomings in constructing a socialist society in Albania. Among other things, the APL proposed that military rank be abolished, political commissars be re-introduced into the armed services, and the salaries of high and middle ranking officials be reduced.[23]

Shortly afterwards, the Albanian cabinet was reduced from 19 to 13 members and the Civil Service was ordered to make substantial cuts in its personnel. In addition, the government promised to take concrete measures to eliminate bureaucratic red tape and to give local political and economic organs a greater degree of freedom.[24] Finally, the regime continued its attacks upon the dissident intellectuals.[25]

In mid-July, while the Cultural Revolution was in full swing, the Central Committee of the APL announced that the Fifth Party Congress would convene on November 1. At the same time the Central Committee made public the results of the Third Five-Year Plan (1961–1965). According to the APL, the objectives of the Plan had "in general been honorably fulfilled." The Party further claimed that 97 per cent of the industrial plan had been realized.[26]

Yet when one examines the results of the Plan, it is

[21] Ibid., February 10, 1966.
[22] Ibid., February 21, 1966.
[23] Ibid., March 6, 1966.
[24] Ibid., March 17, 1966.
[25] See, for example, Zëri i Popullit, June 18, 1966.
[26] Ibid., July 15, 1966.

apparent that it was a gigantic failure. In 1965, industrial production was 39 per cent above the 1960 level. The Plan, however, had foreseen a rise of 52 per cent for the same period. Agricultural output was 36 per cent greater in 1965 than in 1960, but the Plan had predicted that it would be 72 per cent more. Similarly, Albania's national income in 1965 had risen only 32 per cent above the 1960 level instead of the projected 56 per cent.[27] Albania's break with the U.S.S.R. had indeed been costly from the economic standpoint. Yet, as the proceedings of the Fifth Congress of the APL were to demonstrate, Tiranë was in no mood to effect a reconciliation with Moscow.

The Fifth Congress of the Albanian Party of Labor was in session from November 1–8, 1966. There were in attendance 790 delegates representing 66,327 members and candidates of the APL. Of the 31 foreign delegations present, only four (the Chinese, North Korean, North Vietnamese, and Rumanian) represented ruling parties. The remainder were comprised mainly of representatives of the pro-Chinese "Marxist-Leninist" parties.[28]

In his opening address to the Congress, Hoxha made it clear that Albania had no intention of abandoning her pro-Chinese policy and called on "all the Marxist-Leninist Parties and forces" to join Peking and Tiranë in forming a "bloc" to combat the forces of revisionism within the communist camp. According to Hoxha, there could be no neutrals among the communists in the struggle against revisionism. The Albanian Party Secretary also endorsed the Chinese Cultural Revolution, which he termed a "most effective weapon" in the

[27] *Ibid.*
[28] *Ibid.*, November 2, 1966.

177

struggle "to prevent the spread of revisionist and bourgeois ideas."[29]

Hoxha also devoted a substantial portion of his address to the domestic problems confronting Albania. He decried the development of negative phenomena such as the persistence of foreign "bourgeois" and "revisionist" influences in Albanian culture and life, the rise of a free-thinking class of intellectuals who sought to place themselves above party discipline, and the abuses perpetrated against the masses by party and state bureaucrats. He concluded by calling on the people to rededicate themselves to the ideals of the communist revolution.

Prime Minister Shehu, after enthusiastically endorsing the Sino-Albanian alliance, devoted the major portion of his remarks to economic matters.[30] After discussing the difficulties and successes of the Third Five-Year Plan, he announced the major goals of the Fourth Five-Year-Plan (1960–70). Industrial production would be 50–54 per cent greater in 1970 than in 1965, agricultural output was scheduled to rise by 41–46 per cent, and national income was to increase by 45–50 per cent. While lavishly praising the Chinese for the aid they had given Albania in the past, Shehu observed that his country would have to rely increasingly on its own resources in the future. He also revealed that, since the success of the Plan hinged upon the performance of the agricultural sector of the economy, the party would make every effort to correct the problems that persisted in this area.

The Congress concluded by re-electing Enver Hoxha Party Secretary and warmly endorsing his policies.[31]

[29] For the text of Hoxha's address, see *ibid.*
[30] For the text of Shehu's speech, see *ibid.*, November 6, 1966.
[31] Radio Tiranë, November 8, 1966.

There were no significant shifts in the leadership or policies of the APL made at the Fifth Congress. Indeed, the Congress provided convincing evidence of the unity of the Albanian ruling elite and left no doubt that Hoxha and Shehu were still firmly entrenched in power. But the Congress did confirm the negative impact which the Soviet-Albanian break had on the Albanian economy, and demonstrated the deep concern over the social and cultural unrest that had arisen in the country.

Following the conclusion of the Congress, the leaders of the APL continued their efforts to resolve the problems plaguing the nation. On February 6, 1967, Enver Hoxha launched the second phase of the Albanian Cultural Revolution. He urged the people to eliminate all remaining bourgeois traits from Albanian life, and to intensify the struggle against bureaucratism by openly criticizing those party and state officials who abused their power. Hoxha issued a special appeal to the youth of Albania to join in the struggle to preserve the purity of Marxism-Leninism in Albania.[32]

The Albanian Cultural Revolution appears to have reached its peak during the spring and summer of 1967. It was during this period that the Albanian version of the Red Guard was actively engaged in criticizing allegedly delinquent officials, teachers, intellectuals, workers, and ordinary citizens by means of their wall newspapers. Red Guard units were prominent in the anti-religious crusade that swept through Albania at this time, and they also directed their energies along more constructive lines by "volunteering" for work on farms and construction projects.[33] In contrast to their

[32] *Zëri i Popullit*, February 6, 1967.
[33] For the role of the Albanian Red Guard, see *inter alia*, *Zëri i Popullit*, April 1, June 22, September 15, 1967.

Chinese counterparts, the Albanian Red Guard remained under the effective control of the party. Their role, however, appeared to be in eclipse by late 1967.

During the spring and summer of 1967, the Albanian regime also stepped up its campaign to "emancipate" the women of the country.[34] There was a twofold motive for this drive. First, in the face of the labor shortage gripping the country, the state sought to bring as many women as possible into productive work. Second, by bringing the women of the country into the mainstream of Albanian life, it was hoped that they could be persuaded to abandon their conservatism, which was regarded as a major obstacle to the construction of a socialist society.

The impact of the Albanian Cultural Revolution was also felt in the economic sphere. In late April, the government announced a salary reduction for all highly paid workers in an effort to reduce the relatively high standard of living enjoyed by the skilled worker, a situation which had caused some discontent among the lower-paid workers. By taking this step, the government could also devote slightly more of its resources to industrial investment. The government also reduced the size of the private plots on the collective farms and began to agitate for their abolition. To offset the grumbling that was expected to accompany these new policies, the regime proclaimed a retail price cut ranging from 10 to 30 per cent, reduced direct taxes, and promised to increase rural credit and to speed up the process of rural electrification.[35]

Hoping to take advantage of Albania's internal difficulties, the U.S.S.R. during the first half of 1967

[34] *Bashkimi,* June 18, 20, 1967. Women in 1967 comprised 42 per cent of the Albanian labor force. *Ibid.,* June 18, 1967.

[35] Radio Tiranë, April 30, 1967.

sought to improve relations with Tiranë. In late June, the Soviets again offered to resume commercial relations with Albania.[36] Tiranë, however, rejected all Soviet efforts at reconciliation, while the Sino-Albanian alliance remained firm. During 1967, two high ranking Albanian delegations, headed by Defense Minister Beqir Balluku and Prime Minister Mehmet Shehu respectively, visited China. Continuing to stress their common opposition to the policies of the U.S.S.R. and its allies, China and Albania by the end of 1967 stood together and alone among the party states in the vanguard of the anti-Soviet, anti-"revisionist" forces within the communist system.

Summary and Conclusions

Since coming to power in late 1944, the communist rulers of Albania have sought to accomplish three objectives. First, they have been most concerned with maintaining and strengthening their hold on the country. Second, they have striven to preserve the independence and territorial integrity of Albania. Third, they have devoted much effort to the task of modernizing Albania in accordance with the Leninist-Stalinist Soviet model. By capitalizing on the divisions that have arisen in the communist camp since 1948, the Albanian leadership has been able to realize fully the first two of its objectives. The APL, however, has been less successful in achieving its third objective.

In 1948, Hoxha and Shehu were saved from extermination by the Soviet-Yugoslav break. With Russian backing they were able to crush all opposition within the APL. By 1960, their control over the APL

[36] Radio Moscow, June 30, 1967.

181

and Albania was so well established that the Soviet Union, which had by now become disenchanted with the policies of the Albanian leaders, was unable to dislodge them. At this crucial juncture, the Albanians found a new protector, China. This situation, coupled with the pronounced polycentric tendencies that had emerged in the communist system, made it possible for the Albanian leadership to continue to defy the Kremlin with impunity. By the late 1960s the Albanian ruling elite, which was relatively young and highly cohesive, had initiated a "Cultural Revolution" designed to strengthen its influence on all phases of Albanian life.

Albania's rather unique history as a member of the communist system can in large measure be explained by the strong nationalist sentiments of her rulers and people. The Yugoslav-Albanian break of 1948 was precipitated by Tito's attempt to incorporate Albania into Yugoslavia. Again, during the late 1950s and early 1960s the Albanians became alarmed, as Soviet-Yugoslav relations improved, by the fear that Belgrade's price for its reconciliation with Moscow would be the annexation of Albania by Yugoslavia. The vehemence with which the Albanians have waged their campaign against Moscow stems from the belief of their leaders that they are fighting for the preservation of Albania's independence.

Albania's successful defiance of Moscow has resulted in her *de facto* expulsion from the Warsaw Treaty Organization and the Council For Mutual Economic Assistance (COMECON). There have been no formal diplomatic relations between the U.S.S.R. and Albania since December 1961. Albanian ties with the European party states, except for Rumania, continue to be strained. Despite the Soviet-Albanian break and the fact that Albania maintains commercial relations with forty states, approximately 90 per cent of Albania's trade is with communist nations, with China accounting for the bulk of this.

In fact, the major consequence of the Soviet-Albanian break has been the formation of the Sino-Albanian alliance. In recent years, China's ties with Albania have assumed added significance as Peking has experienced difficulties in its relations with the Asian party states and communist parties. Albania not only serves as China's "beachhead" in Europe but also renders valuable service as Peking's chief spokesman in the United Nations. Given the current conditions prevailing in the communist system, it appears unlikely that there will be a significant change in Sino-Albanian relations in the near future.

Albania's break with the U.S.S.R., however, has had a serious and negative impact on the plans of the Albanian leadership to construct a socialist state in accordance with the Soviet model. Owing to the inability of the Chinese to provide the aid needed to achieve this objective, the Albanians, who have been forced to rely more heavily on their own resources, have not been able to industrialize as rapidly as they would like. Furthermore, Albania's balanced economic development has been hindered by the failure of the leadership to resolve the agricultural problem. Unless the Albanian rulers can come up with a solution to the economic problems confronting the nation, they will find their position becoming increasingly difficult.

SELECTED BIBLIOGRAPHY IN ENGLISH

Amery, Julian. *Sons of the Eagle.* London: Macmillan and Co. Ltd., 1948.

Frasheri, Kristo. *The History of Albania: A Brief Survey.* Tiranë: [Naim Frashëri" State Publishing House], 1964.

Gegaj, Athanas, and Krasniqi, Rexhep. *Albania.* New York: Assembly of Captive European Nations, 1964.

Griffith, William E. *Albania and the Sino-Soviet Rift.* Cambridge: The M.I.T. Press, 1963.

Hamm, Harry. *Albania—China's Beachhead in Europe.* Translated by Victor Anderson. New York: Frederick A. Praeger, 1963.

Skendi, Stavro, ed. *Albania.* New York: Frederick A. Praeger, 1958.

————. "Albania." In *The Fate of East Central Europe: Hopes and Failures of American Foreign Policy,* edited by Stephen D. Kertesz. Notre Dame, Ind.: University of Notre Dame Press, 1956.

————. "Albania." In *East Central Europe and the World: Developments in the Post-Stalin Era,* edited by Stephen D. Kertesz. Notre Dame, Ind.: University of Notre Dame Press, 1962.

Tang, Peter S. H. *The Twenty-Second Congress of the Communist Party of the Soviet Union and Moscow-Tirana-Peking Relations.* Washington, D.C.: Research Institute on the Sino-Soviet Bloc, 1962.

Twenty Years of Socialism in Albania. Tiranë: "Naim Frashëri" State Publishing House, 1964.